365 CELLO LESSONS

2007 EDITION

by David Franklin

Lessons and Design Copyright © 2006 by David Franklin

Table of Contents/Preface

Introduction

We're proud to announce some new changes for 2007. In addition to revising this year's edition with over 100 new lessons, we've also revamped the layout, as well as added facts, trivia, and quotes in addition to the daily lessons.

The lessons inside are simple and straightforward, and each one can be completed in five minutes or less. Want to stretch a lesson further? Pressed for time? Use what's presented here as a starting point to modify or supplement as you like.

In the next several pages, you'll find some terms, theory, and other useful information to help you get the most out of this calendar. Read this before starting; it should only take a few minutes.

Got an idea of something you'd like to see in next year's edition? Submit a lesson, and you'll receive a free 2008 calendar!

Thanks for playing!

Useful information

- Some lessons require doing additional research. For example, although we've listed some common chords in this preface, there are plenty more out there. Part of becoming a better player is learning where and how to look for the information you need. Be creative! Libraries, books, music stores, teachers, the Internet, other players, friends, and videos are some places to look. In many cases, we also mention useful links as part of the lesson. For more resources, visit our website: www.Note-A-Day.com.

- Some useful things to have on hand: a metronome; guitar picks; chord books; stereo or boom box; and a journal or notebook.

- For ease of writing, right hand refers to the bowing hand; left hand refers to the fingering hand. If you are a left-handed player, reverse the two.

- While you don't need to be able to read music in order to do the lessons, understanding rhythms will help. See page 13 for more information.

- Focus on the quality of what you're playing. Go slow; make each note count.

- Some lessons involve using your voice; sing an octave lower or higher, as needed.

Glossary

Arpeggio: "broken chord"; playing each note of a chord separately, often sequentially, e.g., C, E, G for a C major chord.

Circle of Fifths: an arrangement of all 12 pitch names that shows any adjacent pair of pitch names (as you move clockwise around the circle) to be a perfect fifth (see page 11).

Improvise: to perform spontaneously, without preparation. To improvise, play a note. Next, play another note. You've just improvised! (OK, so it might not win you the "Player of the Year" award). Improvisation takes practice, and trial and error. If you're new to improvisation, start slowly; your skill will develop over time.

Fret: on some stringed instruments, frets are strips of metal that serve as "built-in" intonation. They also mark each half-step. For ease of reading, we use frets in chord/scale diagrams to mark where each half-step lies.

Plucking: striking a string with the fingers; also called "fingerpicking" or "pizzicato."

Right-hand fingers: letters are sometimes used to abbreviate the fingers: p=thumb, i=index, m=middle, a=ring, e=pinky

Root: the first note when spelling a chord or scale, e.g., C is the root of C major.

3

Anatomy of the Cello/Bow

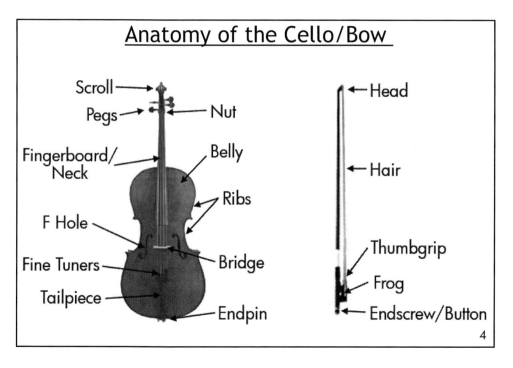

Scroll

Pegs

Nut

Fingerboard/Neck

Belly

Ribs

F Hole

Bridge

Fine Tuners

Tailpiece

Endpin

Head

Hair

Thumbgrip

Frog

Endscrew/Button

4

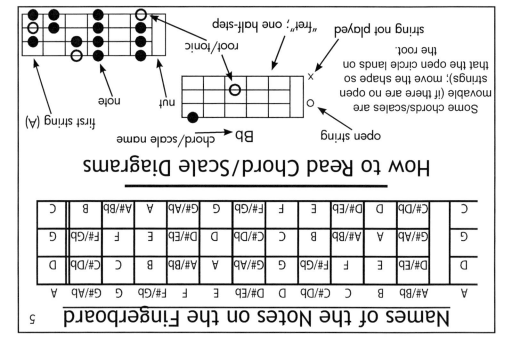

How to Read Chord/Scale Diagrams

- root/tonic
- "fret"; one half-step
- string not played
- that the open circle lands on the root.
- Some chords/scales are movable (if there are no open strings); move the shape so
- open string
- Bb
- chord/scale name
- first string (A)
- note
- nut

Names of the Notes on the Fingerboard

A	A#/Bb	B	C	C#/Db	D	D#/Eb	E	F	F#/Gb	G	G#/Ab	A
D	D#/Eb	E	F	F#/Gb	G	G#/Ab	A	A#/Bb	B	C	C#/Db	D
G	G#/Ab	A	A#/Bb	B	C	C#/Db	D	D#/Eb	E	F	F#/Gb	G
C	C#/Db	D	D#/Eb	E	F	F#/Gb	G	G#/Ab	A	A#/Bb	B	C

Chords

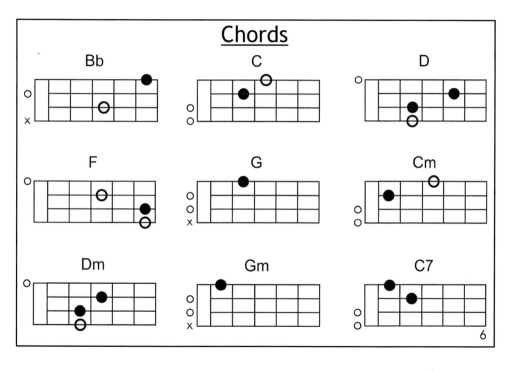

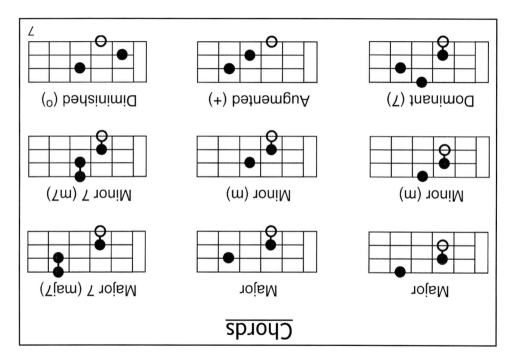

Spelling Scales and Chords

Here are two methods of spelling scales and chords:

1. Use a formula relative to the major scale with the same root:
   The major scale has the formula 1, 2, 3, 4, 5, 6, 7
   The minor scale has the formula 1, 2, b3, 4, 5, b6, b7
   ("b" = down one half-step, "#" = up one half-step)

Start with the major scale, then use the formula. For example, to spell a C minor scale:

C	D	E	F	G	A	B	= C Major scale (refer to Circle of Fifths on page 11)
1	2	3	4	5	6	7	= Major scale formula
1	2	b3	4	5	b6	b7	= minor scale formula
C	D	Eb	F	G	Ab	Bb	= C minor scale

2. Use a formula of half-steps and whole-steps:
   H = half-step = 1 note in the chromatic scale
   W = whole-step = 2 notes in the chromatic scale

Minor scale formula = W H W W H W W

C minor scale = C		D		Eb		F		G		Ab		Bb		C
(formula) =	(W)		(H)		(W)		(W)		(H)		(W)		(H)	

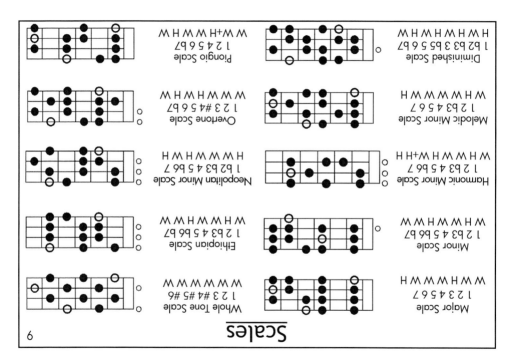

Scales

Major Scale — 1 2 3 4 5 6 7 — W W H W W W H

Minor Scale — 1 2 b3 4 5 b6 b7 — W H W W H W W

Harmonic Minor Scale — 1 2 b3 4 5 b6 7 — W H W W H W+H H

Melodic Minor Scale — 1 2 b3 4 5 6 7 — W H W W W W H

Diminished Scale — 1 b2 b3 3 b5 5 6 b7 — H W H W H W H W

Whole Tone Scale — 1 2 3 #4 #5 #6 — W W W W W W

Ethiopian Scale — 1 2 b3 4 5 b6 b7 — W H W W H W W

Neopolitan Minor Scale — 1 b2 b3 4 5 b6 7 — H W W W H W+H H

Overtone Scale — 1 2 3 #4 5 6 b7 — W W W H W H W

Pfongio Scale — 1 2 4 5 6 7 — W W+H W W W H

Scales

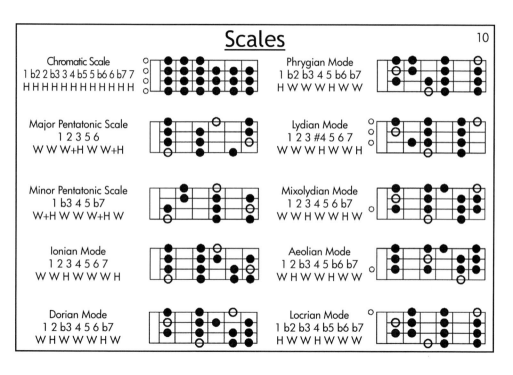

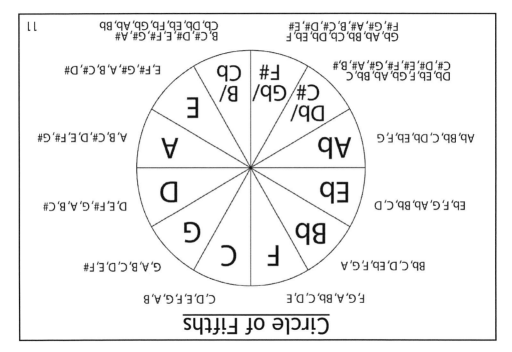

Circle of Fifths

<u>Diatonic Harmony</u>

Diatonic harmony (diatonic: in the key; harmony: the sound of two or more tones simultaneously) shows the chords that go with a key.

To figure out chords in any key or scale, take the notes that are two notes above any note (thirds) and four notes above that same note (fifths) to form a triad. Only use notes that are in the scale.

Here are the chords in C Major:

Original scale (1)	C	D	E	F	G	A	B
Third above note (3 or b3)	E	F	G	A	B	C	D
Fifth above note (5 or b5)	G	A	B	C	D	E	F
Chord quality	M	m	m	M	M	m	°
Corresponding roman numeral	I	ii	iii	IV	V	vi	vii°

In the first column (reading down), C-E-G spells a C Major chord (1-3-5), and is the I chord
In the second column, D-F-A spells a D minor chord (1-b3-5), and is the ii chord
Both of these chords are diatonic to C Major.

Do this in all keys (note that the chord qualities in each major key are the same, e.g., the IV chord is always major, the vi chord always minor, etc.)

Reading Rhythms

While there are many time signatures (numeric indicators of number and length of beats), 4/4 (or C for common time) is the only one used in this calendar. To understand how this works:

Clap evenly, or turn on a metronome. Each clap or click equals one beat. In 4/4 time, four beats equal one measure.

Below are four measures, each separated by a barline. Clap and count 1-2-3-4 for each measure. While clapping, sing "la" for the note written (don't worry about the pitch) when you get to each number. Hold the note that's underlined until you get to the next one.

Whole-notes last for 4 beats = 1 per measure = 1 per every 4 clicks
Half-notes last for 2 beats = 2 per measure = 1 per every 2 clicks
Quarter-notes last for 1 beat = 4 per measure = 1 per every click
Eighth-notes last for 1/2 beat = 8 per measure = 2 per click
Sixteenth-notes last for 1/4 beat = 16 per measure = 4 per click

13

2007
CALENDAR

Note-A-Day
Calendars

Monday
January

1

2007

Write down your musical goals. Create one-month goals, six-month goals, one-year goals, and five-year goals. It might help to think of long-term goals first, then break those down into short-term goals.

On the first day of each month review your goals. Are you on track? Are there any adjustments you need to make in order to reach them? Are there any you want to change? Have you reached any of them?

Update your goals as necessary, and continue to review them each month (there will be a reminder on the page at the beginning of each month).

The cello has a range of C below the bass clef to G at the top of the treble clef.

Note-A-Day
Calendars

Monday

December

31

2007

Reflect back on the previous year, and review your
accomplishments. How have you grown as a player? What have
you learned?

Take time today to appreciate yourself
and celebrate your hard work.

Chordophone is the generic term used for stringed instruments. It refers to
an instrument that is sounded by bowing, plucking, or striking a string that is
stretched between two fixed points.

Tuesday
January
2
2007

Take an open position chord. Move the shape up one half-step, and play all four strings.

Continue moving it up one half-step at a time and playing. Listen to the different sounds you can get from this one shape.

Do this with Cm, Dm, and C7 chord-shapes.

Cm   Dm

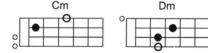

C7

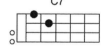

"All music is folk music. I ain't never heard no horse sing a song." - Louis Armstrong

Note-A-Day
Calendars

Sunday
December
30
2007

Improvise, pausing for at least ten seconds
between each note or chord.

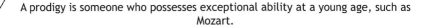

A prodigy is someone who possesses exceptional ability at a young age, such as
Mozart.

Note-A-Day
Calendars

Wednesday
January
3
2007

Play an "Eb". Improvise using the Eb Ionian mode for several minutes.

Occasionally play "Eb" or an Eb arpeggio as a reference for your ears.

A concerto is a composition for, usually, one solo instrument and orchestra.

Note-A-Day

Calendars

Saturday

December

29

2007

Choose a sentence, either one you make up or one from a book, magazine, the Internet, etc.

Improvise and play the sentence on your cello, in whatever way seems right to you. Experiment with different notes and techniques, varying how you play the sentence.

Melody is a musical line produced by a series of song tones.

Note-A-Day
Calendars

Thursday
January
4

2007

Read through the preface in the beginning of the calendar. After reading, do the following:

• Identify where the bridge and nut are on your cello
• Say the names of the open strings
• Play a Dm7 chord
• Spell an A minor scale
• Play the Piongio scale
• Say the notes in a Bb major scale
• Spell a C minor chord
• Clap 3 measures of half-notes in 4/4 time

The term legato means "joined."

Note-A-Day
Calendars

Friday
December
28

2007

Play as fast as you can for five minutes, stopping
as little as possible. Use only improvisation.

"You gotta remember. I'm 24 years old. Who knows if I'm doing what I'm
supposed to be doing? But yeah, I'd like to rock out some day." - Norah Jones

Note-A-Day
Calendars

Friday
January
5

2007

Imagine that today is the last day that you'll ever play your cello again. What would you choose to play or practice? How does imagining this scenario affect your playing?

Five stringed celli were made up until the eighteenth century.

Thursday
December
27

2007

Memorize one scale from the Circle of Fifths (see the preface).
Play it on one string, then using the pattern below.

The Smithsonian's National Museum of American History has the 1701 "Servais"
cello made by Stradivari, uniquely famous for its state of preservation and
musical excellence.

Note-A-Day
Calendars

Saturday
January
6

2007

Memorize and learn to play one new chord today.

Use the preface, or visit http://4stringchords.com.

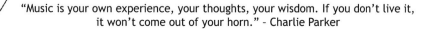

"Music is your own experience, your thoughts, your wisdom. If you don't live it, it won't come out of your horn." - Charlie Parker

Note-A-Day
Calendars

Wednesday
December
26

2007

Check out some free ear-training sites online:

www.good-ear.com
www.ossmann.com/bigears
www.ababasoft.com
www.solfege.org

Practice your ear-training!

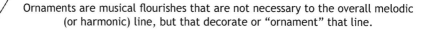

Ornaments are musical flourishes that are not necessary to the overall melodic (or harmonic) line, but that decorate or "ornament" that line.

Practice the following major scale in this manner: ascending and descending in half-notes, then quarter-notes, then eighth-notes.

Next, start on the root and skip to the third note in the scale, back to the second note, skip to the fourth, etc., ascending and descending in all of the above rhythms.

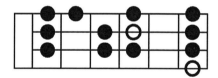

Enharmonic notes are notes that have different names, but have the same pitch, e.g., F# and Gb.

Note-A-Day
Calendars

Tuesday
December
25

2007

Research the history of the cello, such as what similar instruments came before it, when it was created, who created and popularized it, how it's evolved over time, etc.

Free jazz, or avante-garde jazz, is a movement of jazz music characterized by straying from or ignoring formal constraints and structure. It relies upon improvisation, widely varying themes, and unconventional sounds.

Note-A-Day
Calendars

Monday
January

8

2007

Practicing in front of a mirror makes it easier to notice if you need to adjust your posture.

As you practice in front of a mirror, notice your posture. Do you lean to a particular side? Are you slumped in any way? Are you holding the cello correctly?

Strive for an upright yet relaxed posture. Memorize how your body feels when in this posture.

The chromatic scale includes all twelve notes in Western music. It is played sequentially, beginning on any note.

Note-A-Day
Calendars

Monday
December
24

2007

Practice "pull-offs" (legato): place all four left hand fingers down on one string, one half-step apart. Bow the string in one direction, and pull-off your pinky, then pull-off your ring finger, then your middle finger.

Repeat. Make each note equal in volume and quality.

Using a metronome, repeat using whole-, then half- then quarter-, then eighth-, then sixteenth-notes.

"Performers only go wacko when they fall from grace if they like the adulation more than the work." – Meat Loaf

Note-A-Day
Calendars

Tuesday
January

9

2007

Improvise using only notes on the C string.

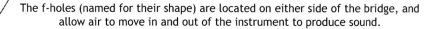

The f-holes (named for their shape) are located on either side of the bridge, and allow air to move in and out of the instrument to produce sound.

Note-A-Day
Calendars

Sunday
December
23
2007

Improvise for 3-5 seconds. Pause for 3-5 seconds, then improvise for 3-5 seconds.

Keep repeating this for several minutes, noticing how leaving space affects what and how you play.

Internally, the cello has two important features: a bass bar, which is glued to the underside of the top of the instrument, and a round wooden sound post (also called a sound peg), which is sandwiched between the top and bottom.

Wednesday
January
10

2007

Memorize the following chord qualities:

add four (add4) (1, 3, 4, 5)
add nine (add9) (1, 3, 5, 9)

Spell each with A as the root (see the preface).

Half-steps are also called semitones.

Saturday
December

22

2007

Memorize the following chord qualities and symbols:

dominant seventh flat five (7b5) (1, 3, b5, b7)
dominant seventh sharp five (7#5) (1, 3, #5, b7)

Spell each with A as the root (see the preface).

An interlude is any piece of music that is played or sung between the movements
of a larger composition.

Note-A-Day
Calendars

Thursday
January

11

2007

Using a tuner, tune your cello.

Memorize the pitch of one note, to the point where you can hear and sing it without playing it first.

Use this note when you don't have a tuner to bring your cello up to pitch, or as a reference to help figure out other pitches.

The four types of triads are: major, minor, augmented, and diminished.

Note-A-Day
Calendars

Friday
December

21

2007

Improvise using chords.

Using C, F, and G chords, improvise for five minutes. Experiment
with playing only part of the chord, reverse bowing, varying
tempos, rhythms, etc.

Be creative - feel free to use whatever ideas you like.

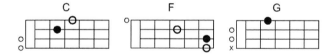

A mazurka, like the waltz, has three beats, but the accent is on the second beat
rather than the first.

Friday
January
12
2007

Practice the following minor scale in this manner: ascending and descending in half-notes, then quarter-notes, then eighth-notes.

Next, start on the root and skip to the third note in the scale, back to the second note, skip to the fourth, etc., ascending and descending in all of the above rhythms.

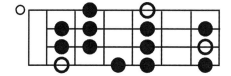

The term "comping" is jazz jargon for accompanying.

Play the following minor pentatonic scale.

Play it again, singing each note as you play it - use the syllables do (1), mi (3), fa (4), sol (5), ti (7), do (8), with each syllable corresponding to the note in the scale.

Thursday
December
20

2007

Next, play the root (first) note. Sing the second note (using re), then play the third note. Sing the fourth note (using sol), play the fifth, etc., ascending and descending.

John Phillip Sousa's "Washington Post" sparked the dance craze known as the two-step.

Note-A-Day
Calendars

Saturday
January

13

2007

Memorize and learn to play one new chord today.

Use the preface, or visit http://4stringchords.com.

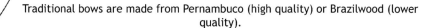

Traditional bows are made from Pernambuco (high quality) or Brazilwood (lower quality).

Wednesday
December

19

2007

Play each of the following chords as an arpeggio (one note at a time, in order):

dominant seventh flat five (7b5) (1, 3, b5, b7)
dominant seventh sharp five (7#5) (1, 3, #5, b7)

Play each with D as the root (see the preface).
Pay attention to the sound of each arpeggio.

The hair of the bow is coated with rosin to make it grip the strings and cause them to vibrate.

Without looking at your cello, name all of the strings and "frets" where the following notes are found (e.g., Db is 4th string-1st "fret", 3rd string-6th "fret", etc.):
Eb, D, Ab, F#

Sunday
January

14

2007

Set your metronome to 60 bpm. Starting from the fourth string and moving one string at a time to the first, say which "fret" the note appears on with each click.

Do this separately with each of the notes above.

"The important thing is to feel your music, really feel it and believe it." – Ray Charles

Note-A-Day
Calendars

Tuesday
December
18

2007

Create your own open tuning. Tune the open strings until you get
a sound that you like.

Experiment and improvise using this tuning. See
how quickly you can tune between this tuning
and standard tuning without using a tuner.

"It's taken me all my life to learn what not to play." - Dizzy Gillespie

Note-A-Day
Calendars

See what kinds of sounds you can create using the following techniques:

• Tapping or drumming on the body, neck, or scroll (experiment with different locations, fingers, etc.)
• Playing the strings by the scroll (behind the nut)
• Pulling the high or low strings off of the fingerboard, then playing (pull off at different locations)
• Fingering notes (pressing on the strings) over the soundhole and playing
• Scraping the strings with your nails

Come up with your own unorthodox techniques!

Monday
January
15

2007

Grace notes are short notes played just before the main note of a tune as an ornament.

Monday
December

17

2007

Play an F chord. First ascending, then descending, play each note of the chord and sing it, using the syllable "la" (changing octaves as needed).

Play and sing the lowest note of the chord, then sing (without playing, ascending then descending) the rest of the notes.

Do this for G and Bb chords as well.

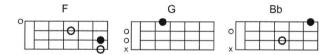

Mozart wrote a musical dice game where each measure is numbered, and the order of performance is dictated by the results of throws of the dice.

Tuesday
January
16

2007

Play the following pattern across all four strings (play on the fourth string, then the third, then second, etc.) without stopping (numbers correspond to the "frets"):

7-9-11-12

Play evenly and slowly, with four notes per click of the metronome (sixteenth-notes). Gradually speed up the tempo.

To modulate is to move from one key to another.

Sunday
December
16
2007

Play an "Eb". Improvise using the Eb major scale for several minutes.

Occasionally play "Eb" as a reference note for your ears.

Next, improvise using the Eb minor scale for several minutes.

When you feel comfortable, continue improvising and moving back and forth between the two scales.

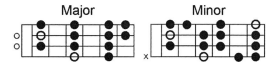

The elements of rhythm are meter (the basic pulse) and accentuation (emphasis on one part of a phrase).

Wednesday
January
17

2007

Practice playing natural harmonics: while bowing close to the bridge, lightly touch the fourth string in the first position and slide your finger up the string. Listen to the different harmonics that are produced, and notice where the harmonics sound clearest.

Do this on each string, memorizing the areas and pitches where you get the clearest sounds.

Some professionals believe that eventually bow hair can "lose its grip." Others disagree, saying that if the ribbon has enough hair and tightens properly, a proper cleaning will restore its playing quality.

Note-A-Day
Calendars

Saturday
December

15

2007

Quality of practice yields more results than quantity. Fifteen minutes of focused practicing is more effective than one hour of noodling.

Make sure you are in a space where you can be completely uninterrupted from phones, children, TVs, etc. and stay focused on your music.

Originally, the cello's light sound was not as suitable for church and ensemble playing, so it had to be doubled by basses or violins.

Thursday
January
18

2007

Learn and experiment with the Neopolitan Minor scale:
1, b2, b3, 4, 5, b6, 7

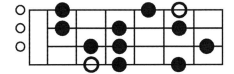

A pentatonic scale is made up of five, rather than seven, notes between octaves.

Practice trills. Hold one finger down and rapidly and repeatedly hammer-on and pull-off another finger while moving the bow in one direction.

Friday
December

14

2007

Start with your index finger down and trilling with your middle finger, then ring, then pinky, one-two-three half-steps above, respectively. Take time to do each combination separately. Then hold your middle finger down and trill with your ring, then pinky. Last, hold down your ring finger and trill with your pinky.

See how long you can trill on each finger without stopping - this is a great way to build speed and endurance.

A theme is a melody, usually repeated, that forms a building block of a piece.

Note-A-Day
Calendars

Friday
January

19

2007

Create a five-minute warm-up routine. Use it to help avoid injury and get the most out of your practice time.

You might start with stretching your body, arms, and hands, then playing some scales (very slowly, building up speed), some basic chords (both as block chords and as arpeggios), then some slow improvisation.

Always start slowly, paying attention to the tone and quality of what you're playing. Use this routine each time you practice or perform.

"Music is just a means of creating a magical state." – Robert Fripp

Play an "Eb". Improvise using the Eb Dorian mode for several minutes.

Occasionally play "Eb" or an Ebm arpeggio as a reference for your ears.

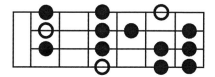

A banner at New York's Lincoln Center for the Performing Arts once read "Savage Beasts Soothed Here."

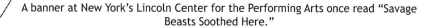

Play the minor scale below, accenting every third note (to accent, play the note with a little more emphasis than the others).

Do this ascending and descending in quarter-notes and eighth-notes.

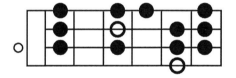

The term rubato means not strictly in tempo—played freely and expressively.

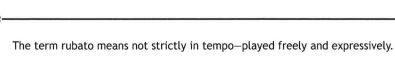

Note-A-Day
Calendars

Wednesday
December
12
2007

Transcribe a song that you like from a recording. Take a minimum of five minutes; see how much you can figure out.

The first American-made recording of an orchestra was in 1917 by The Boston Symphony Orchestra.

Note-A-Day
Calendars

Sunday
January
21

2007

Learn how to maintain and care for your cello.

Visit the library, and/or try typing "cello care" into a search engine (www.PottersViolins.com is also a good resource).

The cello reaches the lowest pitch in the traditional string quartet and is capable of covering nearly the entire range of pitches produced by the human voice.

Tuesday
December

11

2007

Memorize how to spell the minor pentatonic scale (see the preface).

Memorize and play the Db minor pentatonic scale on the fourth string only, then play it using the pattern below.

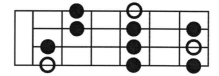

Arguably, the bow is the major determinant in the expressiveness of cello playing.

Note-A-Day
Calendars

Monday
January
22

2007
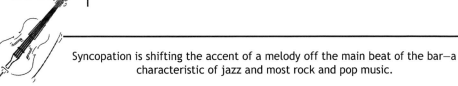

Play each of the following chords as an arpeggio (one note at a time, in order):

augmented (aug or +) (1, 3, #5)
diminished (dim or °) (1, b3, b5)

Play each with D as the root (see the preface).
Pay attention to the sound of each arpeggio.

Syncopation is shifting the accent of a melody off the main beat of the bar—a characteristic of jazz and most rock and pop music.

Note-A-Day
Calendars

Monday
December
10
2007

Memorize and learn to play one new chord today.

Use the preface, or visit http://4stringchords.com.

The first phonograph (a device for recording and replaying sound) was unveiled
on November 21, 1877 by Thomas Edison.

Note-A-Day
Calendars

Tuesday
January
23

2007

Play a 12-bar blues chord progression. Play each chord once per measure as an arpeggio, using whatever rhythms you choose.

Use the following progression (read left to right):

Eb	Ab	Eb	Eb
Ab	Ab	Eb	Eb
Bb	Ab	Eb	Bb

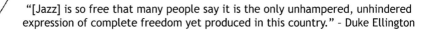

"[Jazz] is so free that many people say it is the only unhampered, unhindered expression of complete freedom yet produced in this country." – Duke Ellington

Practice the following minor pentatonic scale in the following rhythms, ascending and descending: whole-, half-, quarter-, and eighth-notes.

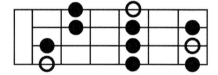

In many modern concert halls, the sound is as good or better in the upper sections as it is in the front row.

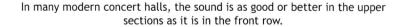

Calendars

Wednesday

January

24

2007

Common sense is that if you're having trouble playing something, try playing it much slower. However, many musicians will keep trying to play the phrase or song at the same speed, even if they keep messing up!

So, if you're having trouble playing something correctly, slow it down!

The word timbre (French, pronounced like the first two syllables of tambourine) refers to the quality of a musical note, or different types of sound production on musical instruments.

Note-A-Day
Calendars

Saturday
December
8

2007

Practice "hammer-ons" (legato): Place your index finger on one note. Bowing in one direction, place your middle finger one half-step above, then your ring finger one half-step above that, then your pinky one half-step above your ring finger.

Repeat. Make each note equal in volume and quality.

Using a metronome, repeat using whole-, half- quarter-, eighth-, and sixteenth-notes.

Benny Goodman made front-page news in 1938 when his swing band played Carnegie Hall, then a strictly classical institution.

Thursday
January
25
2007

Choose a scale that you know how to play.

Counting the first note (tonic) as "one," count two notes above the tonic (staying in the scale), then four notes above the tonic (staying in the scale). Take those three notes and form a chord.

Next, start with the second note in the scale, and do the same thing: count two notes above it, then four notes above it, and create a chord.

Do this for each note in the scale. When you finish, you'll have seven chords, one for each note in the scale (this is also called "diatonic harmony" - see the preface). You can play the original scale over any of the seven chords you created.

Tone production and volume of sound depend on a combination of several factors. The three most important ones are: bow speed, arm weight applied to the string, and point of contact of the bow hair with the string.

Note-A-Day
Calendars

Friday
December

7

2007

List your cello influences. What about them do you admire and appreciate? What qualities of theirs would you like to possess? How did they get where they are as players?

Pick one influence, and pretend to be that person while you play. How do you feel when you imagine yourself as that person?

Mimic him or her while you play, emphasizing personality and expression.

The fifth of Bach's "6 Suites for Unaccompanied Cello" requires an altered tuning of the strings, known as scordatura.

Friday
January

26

2007

Choose an open position chord. Move the shape up one half-step, and play all four strings.

Continue moving it up one half-step at a time and playing. Listen to the different sounds you can get from this one shape.

Do this with F, G, and Bb chord-shapes.

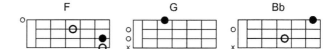

The patron saint of music is St. Cecilia.

Note-A-Day
Calendars

Thursday
December
6
2007

At night, turn off all of the lights in your practice space. In complete darkness, improvise.

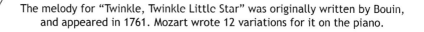

The melody for "Twinkle, Twinkle Little Star" was originally written by Bouin, and appeared in 1761. Mozart wrote 12 variations for it on the piano.

Note-A-Day
Calendars

Saturday
January
27
2007

Some recommended books:

"Art of Cello Playing" by Louis Potter, Jr.

"The Gig Bag Book of Theory and Harmony" by Mark Bridges and Joe Dineen

"Tipbook - Cello" by Hugo Pinksterboer

"Casals and the Art of Interpretation" by David Blum

"Essential Elements for Strings: Cello" by Michael Allen et al.

"The Songwriter's Idea Book" by Sheila Davis

Chamber music is defined as music suitable for performance in a room or small hall, e.g., music for quartets or other small ensembles.

Note-A-Day
Calendars

Improvise using only notes on the first, second, and fourth strings.

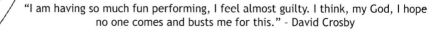

"I am having so much fun performing, I feel almost guilty. I think, my God, I hope no one comes and busts me for this." – David Crosby

Sunday
January
28

2007

Practice improvising to different beats. While tapping your foot very slowly, improvise.

After a minute, tap your foot twice as fast and improvise.

Lastly, tap your foot twice as fast as before, continuing to improvise.

Notice how each type of beat affects how you play.

In addition to piano, R&B legend Ray Charles played trumpet, saxophone, clarinet, and organ.

Note-A-Day
Calendars

Tuesday

December

4

2007

Play any chord. After playing it once, play any note (in the chord or not). Listen to how that note sounds with the chord (you can stop the chord from ringing and hear it in your mind if necessary).

Do this with at least five different notes. Use this exercise to train your ears to learn how different notes sound with different chords.

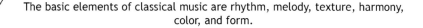

The basic elements of classical music are rhythm, melody, texture, harmony, color, and form.

Note-A-Day
Calendars

Monday
January

29

2007

Record yourself playing a song that you are working on. Listen back to it, and, as objectively as possible, critique your playing (both positives and negatives). It might help to imagine that you are listening to someone else.

Use these observations to improve.

Because of the enormous range of the instrument, written music for the cello frequently alternates between the bass clef, tenor clef, and treble clef.

Note-A-Day
Calendars

Monday
December
3
2007

Practice tremolo or sautillé stroke. Play an open string as rapidly as possible, letting your wrist do the work (not your arm).

Practice this on different strings.

The cellos of the 17th- and 18th-century masters (e.g., Stradivari and Guarneri) tend to be slightly smaller than what is today considered full-sized.

Tuesday
January
30

2007

Choose a song you can play well. Play it while holding the cello in different positions, such as lying down, standing up, even behind your head! Come up with some more positions on your own.

Experiment and have fun! Notice how you feel as you play in each position.

A chord whose notes are played simultaneously is known as a block, flat, or solid chord. A chord whose notes are played separately or in a series is known as a broken or rolled chord, or an arpeggio.

Note-A-Day
Calendars

Sunday
December
2

2007

Research different cello manufacturers and luthiers.
Notice their different philosophies and styles, and
what distinguishes them from each other.

An overture (French, ouverture, meaning opening) is the instrumental
introduction to a dramatic, choral, or (occasionally) instrumental composition.

Note-A-Day
Calendars

Wednesday
January
31
2007

Journal for at least five minutes on why you play the cello, what it means to you, and how it affects your life.

Some questions to guide you: What about playing do you enjoy? Do you play for yourself, or because other people want you to? Are you wanting recognition, appreciation, and/or to prove something? How does playing make your life better? Do you pressure yourself to practice, or practice an amount that feels good to you? What or who inspired you to play the cello? Do you have any dreams related to playing?

Feel free to come up with your own questions as well, either in place of or in addition to the above questions. See what you learn and notice by doing this.

Hardcore punk (or hardcore) is a faster and heavier version of punk rock. It is usually characterized by short, loud, and often passionate songs with exceptionally fast tempos and chord changes.

Note-A-Day
Calendars

Play each of the following chords as an arpeggio (one note at a time, in order):

major ninth (maj9) (1, 3, 5, 7, 9)
minor ninth (m9) (1, b3, 5, b7, 9)

Play each with D as the root (see the preface).
Pay attention to the sound of each arpeggio.

Review your musical goals today.

Thursday
February
1

2007

Practice clapping eighth-note triplets. Set the metronome to 60 bpm, and clap three notes for every click of the metronome, making sure each note lasts for the same amount of time. Say "tri-pl-et" as you clap, with each syllable corresponding to each clap.

When you feel comfortable with this, try quarter-note triplets, clapping three notes for every two clicks of the metronome (hint: still say "tri-pl-et" as before, but only clap the "tri" and "et" for the first click, and on the "pl" after the second click).

Review your musical goals today.

Note-A-Day
Calendars

Friday
November

30

2007

Research the differences between equal temperament intonation and Pythagoras intonation (www.ViolinMasterclass.com/intonation.php is a good resource).

"A Colour Symphony," written by Sir Arthur Bliss, evokes specific colors through sound.

Friday
February

2

2007

Research the cello's role in each of the five main eras of classical music (Renaissance, Baroque, Classical, Romantic, and Modern).

A wolf tone, or simply a "wolf", is a noise that is produced when a note played on a stringed instrument matches the natural resonating frequency of the instrument, producing a tone that is loud and harsh.

Thursday
November

29

2007

Some tips for transcribing:

- Use headphones
- Try to determine the key of the song; identify as many individual notes as possible, and figure out what key they belong to
- If possible, listen to different recordings of the song and/or find a live video
- Use a good pencil and eraser
- Use a CD player or computer program with a cue feature to quickly scan back and forth

Humidifiers are used to control and stabilize the humidity around and inside the cello.

Play an "Ab". Improvise using the Ab Lydian mode for several minutes.

Saturday
February
3
2007

Occasionally play "Ab" or an Ab arpeggio as a reference for your ears.

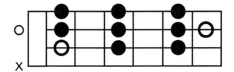

A claque is a group of people in an audience who are paid to applaud loudly.

Note-A-Day
Calendars

Wednesday
November

28

2007

Practice writing the following symbols:
whole-note rest; half-note rest; quarter-note rest; eighth-note rest;
sixteenth-note rest.
Write each at least five times.

An oratorio is a large musical composition for orchestra, vocal soloists, and chorus. It differs from an opera in that it does not have scenery, costumes, or acting.

Play an "Eb". Improvise using the Eb Mixolydian mode for several minutes.

Occasionally play "Eb" or an Eb7 arpeggio as a reference for your ears.

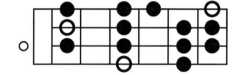

Classical music is defined as any highly evolved music that is written down, as opposed to folk or popular music, which is usually passed down orally. It is also known as "serious," highbrow," "cultivated," or "art" music.

Note-A-Day
Calendars

Tuesday
November
27
2007

Memorize how to spell the major scale (see the preface).

Memorize and play the Ab major scale the third string only, then play it using the pattern below.

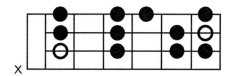

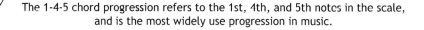

The 1-4-5 chord progression refers to the 1st, 4th, and 5th notes in the scale, and is the most widely use progression in music.

Monday
February
5

2007

Learn to recognize the sound of major, minor, and dominant chords.

Play each of the chords below, listening to the differences between each one. If possible, sing all of the notes of each chord to help learn the sound.

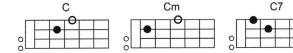

Coda is Italian for "tail."

Monday
November
26
2007

Find another musician (not a cellist) and make a date to play together.

See what you can come up with and create.
Improvise, write songs, share ideas, etc.

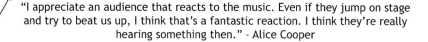

"I appreciate an audience that reacts to the music. Even if they jump on stage and try to beat us up, I think that's a fantastic reaction. I think they're really hearing something then." – Alice Cooper

Note-A-Day

Calendars

Tuesday
February

6

2007

When you can play something perfectly five times in a row, you have mastered it and are ready to move on. If you make a mistake, even on the fifth time, go back to the beginning and start again. Apply this to everything you practice.

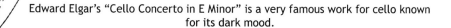

Edward Elgar's "Cello Concerto in E Minor" is a very famous work for cello known for its dark mood.

Note-A-Day
Calendars

Sunday
November
25

2007

Choose a movie or TV show that you like
and learn the theme on cello.

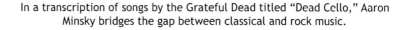

In a transcription of songs by the Grateful Dead titled "Dead Cello," Aaron
Minsky bridges the gap between classical and rock music.

Note-A-Day Calendars

Wednesday
February
7
2007

Memorize the names of the letters for the right-hand fingers:

p = thumb, i = index, m = middle, a = ring

Finger an F major chord and pluck in the following order: p (on 4th string), i (3rd string), m (2nd string), a (1st), m (2nd), i (3rd).

Practice this using different rhythms.

F

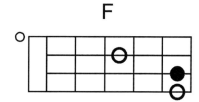

"Music was my refuge. I could crawl into the space between the notes and curl my back to loneliness." – Maya Angelou

Note-A-Day

Calendars

Saturday
November
24
2007

Improvise using only your left hand.

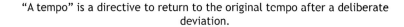

"A tempo" is a directive to return to the original tempo after a deliberate deviation.

Note-A-Day
Calendars

Thursday
February
8
2007

Pick a spot in your house where you don't usually sit, such as in a hallway, kitchen, bathroom, etc. Practice in that spot.

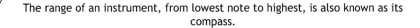

The range of an instrument, from lowest note to highest, is also known as its compass.

Note-A-Day
Calendars

Friday
November

23

2007

Practice the Db melodic minor scale (1, 2, b3, 4, 5, 6, 7) in this manner: ascending and descending in half-notes, then quarter-notes, then eighth-notes.

Next, start on the root and skip to the third note in the scale, back to the second note, skip to the fourth, etc., ascending and descending in all of the above rhythms.

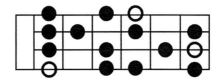

"I have always had a certain song in my head, a certain chemistry of sounds."
- Bjork

Note-A-Day

Calendars

Friday
February

9

2007

Play the major pentatonic scale below.

Play it again, singing each note as you play it - use the syllables do (1), re (2), mi (3), sol (5), la (6), do (8), with each syllable corresponding to the note in the scale.

Next, play the root (first) note. Sing that note, then sing (without playing) the entire scale, ascending and descending.

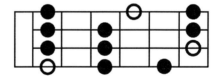

The term "recital" for a solo concert was invented by Franz Liszt's London manager, and its use became popular in the 19th century.

Note-A-Day Calendars

Thursday
November
22

2007

Rosin makes the hair of the bow stick to the string and produce vibration and tone.

Too little rosin leads to using extra weight and tension, causing fatigue and poor tone. Too much rosin can also cause poor tone, as well as damage the wood.

Experiment with different amounts of rosin, finding a good balance.

Al fresco, Italian for "in the open air," is a term for outdoor concerts. They are usually free of charge.

Note-A-Day
Calendars

Saturday
February

10

2007

Play an "Eb". Improvise using the Eb Lydian mode for several minutes.

Occasionally play "Eb" or an Eb arpeggio as a reference for your ears.

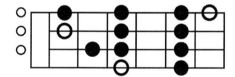

Pablo Casals is best remembered for his recording of Bach's Cello Suites, recorded from 1936 to 1939.

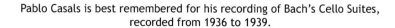

Play an "Eb". Improvise using the Eb Phrygian mode for several minutes.

Occasionally play "Eb" or an Ebm arpeggio as a reference for your ears.

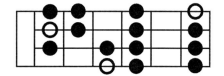

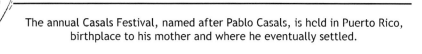

The annual Casals Festival, named after Pablo Casals, is held in Puerto Rico, birthplace to his mother and where he eventually settled.

Play a D augmented chord.

Improvise a melody over it with your voice, playing
the chord only when you can't hear it any longer.
Do this for at least several minutes.

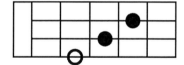

Concert pitch was not standardized until the early 20th century. In fact, it has
risen slightly over time. A symphony composed in Mozart's time sounds one half-
step higher now than it did then.

Tuesday
November
20
2007

Improvise, using only notes on the second and fourth strings.

Perfect pitch is the ability to identify a given pitch without reference to any other pitch.

Monday
February
12

2007

Some inspiring cello albums to check out:

Vivaldi's Cello (Yo-Yo Ma)

Bach: Suites for Solo Cello (Janos Starker)

Cello Blue (David Darling)

Brahms: Cello Sonatas (Mstislav Rostropovich)

Dvořák, Tchaikovsky, Borodin: Quartets (Emerson String Quartet)

Jazz Cello (Ray Brown)

Forever Cello (Marston Smith)

Shostakovich: Cello Concertos Nos. 1 & 2 (Maria Kliegel)

The concert pianist Paul Wittgenstein commissioned many concertos for left hand only after losing his right arm in World War I.

Monday
November

19

2007

Play each of the following chords as an arpeggio (one note at a time, in order):

eleventh (11) (1, 3, 5, 7,11)
thirteenth (13) (1, 3, 5, 7,13)

Play each with D as the root (see the preface).
Pay attention to the sound of each arpeggio.

"You can play a shoestring if you're sincere." - John Coltrane

Play an "Eb". Improvise using the Eb Locrian mode for several minutes.

Occasionally play "Eb" or an Eb diminished arpeggio as a reference for your ears.

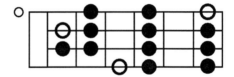

The word "music" is originally derived from the Greek mousa, or muse.

Note-A-Day
Calendars

Sunday
November
18
2007

Tune your cello to "open C" tuning: C, G, E, G (low to high).

Experiment and improvise using this tuning. See
how quickly you can tune between this tuning
and standard tuning without using a tuner.

Acid rock is a genre of American rock that emerged in the late 1960s. Its
style features heavy amplification, instrumental improvisation, new sound
technologies, and light shows.

Wednesday
February

14

2007

Play and sing any note.

Next, play that note and the note one half-step above it. Sing the first note, then the second.

Play the original note, then the one below it. Sing the first note, then the second.

Repeat, each time moving one half-step higher or lower from the original note.

Cello concerti have been written since the time of Vivaldi and Tartini, and possibly earlier.

Note-A-Day Calendars

Practice memorizing and playing the following intervals (an interval is the distance between two notes).

major sixth (M6); 4-½ steps or 9 "frets"; Example: D to Bb
major seventh (M7); 5-½ steps or 11 "frets"; Example: Db to C

Saturday
November
17
2007

Play the higher note, then the lower note. Sing both. Play both notes simultaneously. Sing both. Memorize the sound.

M6

M7

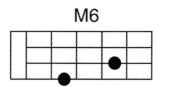

Édouard Lalo's Cello "Concerto in D minor" is his only cello concerto. The piece was written in 1876, inspired by "Camille Saint-Saëns' Cello Concerto in A minor."

Thursday
February

15

2007

Play a major scale. While playing the scale, sing the note that is four notes below the one you are playing (while staying in the scale). Tip: first play the note you'll be singing to learn the pitch, then go back and play the first note while singing the second one.

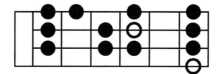

"Music must never forget itself, it must never cease to be music." - Wolfgang Amadeus Mozart

Play an "Ab". Improvise using the Ab Mixolydian mode for several minutes.

Occasionally play "Ab" or an Ab7 arpeggio as a reference for your ears.

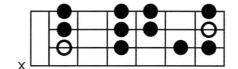

When notating music, notes above "B" are written with the stem pointing downward. Notes below (and including) "B" are written with the stem pointing upward.

Note-A-Day
Calendars

Friday
February

16

2007

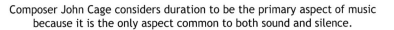

Improvise, imitating a brass or woodwind player. Every time you play, blow out. When you run out of breath, stop playing, inhale, then start again. You can also stop before you run out of breath.

Composer John Cage considers duration to be the primary aspect of music because it is the only aspect common to both sound and silence.

Note-A-Day
Calendars

Thursday
November
15
2007

Look up and memorize definitions for the following musical styles
(www.8notes.com/glossary is a good resource):
gigue, bourée, caprice, rondo, fugue, prelude

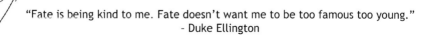

"Fate is being kind to me. Fate doesn't want me to be too famous too young."
- Duke Ellington

Note-A-Day
Calendars

Saturday
February

17

2007

Play a note. Listen to it intently, focusing all your attention
on the sound. Listen for when the note completely
fades away; as soon as it does, play and repeat.

Music is called "traditional" when the composer is no longer known.

Practice the following minor pentatonic scale in
the following rhythms, ascending and descending:
whole-, half-, quarter-, and eighth-notes.

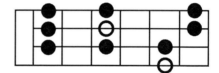

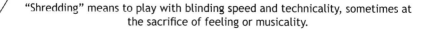

"Shredding" means to play with blinding speed and technicality, sometimes at
the sacrifice of feeling or musicality.

Sunday
February

18

2007

Play an "Ab". Improvise using the Ab major scale for several minutes.

Occasionally play "Ab" as a reference note for your ears.

Play "Ab" again, then improvise using the Ab minor scale for several minutes.

When you feel comfortable, continue improvising and moving back and forth between the two scales.

Major

Minor

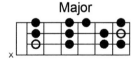

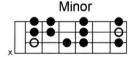

The Beatles pioneered the use of a solo cello in popular music in songs such as "Eleanor Rigby."

Note-A-Day
Calendars

Tuesday
November
13
2007

Play each of the following chords as an arpeggio (one note at a time, in order):

major seventh (maj7) (1, 3, 5, 7)
minor seventh (m7) (1, b3, 5, b7)

Play each with D as the root (see the preface).
Pay attention to the sound of each arpeggio.

Established non-traditional cello groups include Apocalyptica, a group of Finnish cellists best known for their versions of heavy metal songs, and Rasputina, a group of three female cellists who play intricate Gothic music.

Monday
February
19

2007

Play each of the following chords as an arpeggio (one note at a time, in order):

major (M) (1, 3, 5)
minor (m) (1, b3, 5)

Play each with D as the root (see the preface).
Pay attention to the sound of each arpeggio.

Beethoven quit school at age eleven.

Note-A-Day
Calendars

Monday
November

12

2007

Play a note on the cello. Sing it.

Sing it again, saying the name of the note.

Do this with six notes.

Lines above or below the staff are called ledger lines.

Note-A-Day
Calendars

Tuesday
February
20
2007

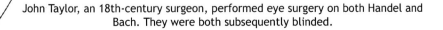

Memorize and learn to play one new chord today.

Use the preface, or visit http://4stringchords.com.

John Taylor, an 18th-century surgeon, performed eye surgery on both Handel and Bach. They were both subsequently blinded.

Note-A-Day
Calendars

Play the following pattern on the first string (A) (numbers correspond to both the "frets" and fingers). Play evenly and slowly, with four notes per click of the metronome (sixteenth-notes):

1-3-2-4

Play the pattern once, then move it up one half-step at a time, ending when you reach the 10th "fret". Then, move back down to the first "fret", one half-step at a time.

"Rock's so good to me. Rock is my child and my grandfather." - Chuck Berry

Note-A-Day
Calendars

Wednesday
February
21

2007

Make a random chord shape using two fingers. Move the shape up one half-step, and play all four strings.

Continue moving it up one half-step at a time and playing. Listen to the different sounds you can get from this one shape.

Schumann showed great promise as a pianist, until his own hand-strengthening device damaged two fingers on his right hand.

Saturday
November

10

2007

Play a C major chord.

Improvise a melody over it with your voice.
Do this for at least several minutes.

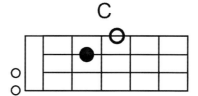

A false note is a muted or dampened note that has no discernible pitch.

Note-A-Day
Calendars

Thursday
February
22

2007

Taking a break from your instrument can help you return with a fresh perspective, increased energy, and new inspiration, among other things.

Take the day off from practicing or playing today, or even thinking about your cello. If you find yourself thinking about it, see if you can turn your attention to something else.

The Nebraskan band Cursive used a cello to make their guitar and cello harmonies on their album, "The Ugly Organ."

Practice the following major scale in this manner: ascending and descending in half-notes, then quarter-notes, then eighth-notes.

Next, start on the root and skip to the third note in the scale, back to the second note, skip to the fourth, etc., ascending and descending in all of the above rhythms.

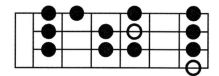

David Tecchler was an Austrian luthier, best known for his cellos and double basses. A 1706 Tecchler cello was acquired by the Canada Council for the Arts Musical Instrument Bank and is on loan to Canadian cellist Denis Brott.

Note-A-Day
Calendars

Friday
February
23

2007

Taking one "fret" at a time, name all of the notes on the 4th, 6th, 8th, 10th, and 11th "frets", starting from the fourth string and moving towards the first (e.g., for the open strings, it would be C, G, D, A).

J.S. Bach once walked 30 miles to hear a performance by organist J.A. Reinkin. He then walked over 200 miles to hear organist Dietrich Buxtehude.

Note-A-Day
Calendars

Thursday
November
8
2007

Choose one note. Bow it for as long as possible, letting it ring afterwards. Feel the vibration of the note in your body. Listen to the quality of the note.

When the note fades away, play again and repeat, feeling it in different parts of your body.

In written music, 5:4 means that five notes are played in the space of four notes. Sometimes, just the first number is used for simplification.

List of things to bring to a gig:

- An extra set of strings
- Small flashlight
- Business cards and promotional materials
- Tuner
- Sheet music and stand
- Accessories: extra bows, nail files, rosin, etc.
- Directions, contact info, and maps

The note that begins a scale is called a keynote, or tonic.

Note-A-Day
Calendars

Wednesday
November
7

2007

Memorize the diatonic chords (see the preface) for minor keys:

i = minor
ii° = diminished
III = Major
iv = minor
v = minor
VI = Major
VII = Major

Studio musicians often have to read music on the first take without ever having seen it before.

Sunday
February

25

2007

Play a C7 chord.

Improvise a melody over it with your voice, playing
the chord only when you can't hear it any longer.
Do this for at least several minutes.

C7

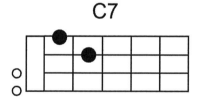

The symbols for flat (b) and sharp (#) are called chromatic signs, or accidentals
when applied.

Note-A-Day
Calendars

Tuesday
November
6

2007

The I-vi-IV-V chord progression is very common in oldies music.
Learn to play and recognize the sound of it.

Two progressions to practice with are C-Am-F-G and G-Em-C-D.

Decay is the physical process by which a sound gradually disappears from the
audible spectrum until it no longer exists.

Finger an F major chord and pluck in the following order: p (on the 4th string), a (1st string), m (2nd string), i (3rd), m (2nd), a (1st).

Practice this using different rhythms.

Monday
February
26

2007

F

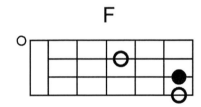

Aaron Minsky (or stage name Von Cello) began his career as a rock guitarist and was influenced by guitarists like Jimi Hendrix, Frank Zappa, and Jerry Garcia. During high school he transferred his knowledge of rock guitar to the cello.

Note-A-Day
Calendars

Monday
November
5

2007

Research the cello's role in different musical genres,
including popular, classical, bluegrass, and jazz
music (http://wikipedia.org is a great resource).

There have been several pieces written for cello ensembles of up to twenty or
more cellists.

Tuesday
February
27

2007

Visit http://4stringchords.com, and use it as a tool to
help learn new chords. Research other chord sites
by typing "cello chords" into a search engine.

An interval is the difference in pitch between two notes.

Sunday
November
4

2007

Improvise using only notes on the A string.

"My sole inspiration is a telephone call from a director." - Cole Porter

Note-A-Day
Calendars

Play an "Ab". Improvise using the Ab Phrygian mode for several minutes.

Occasionally play "Ab" or an Abm arpeggio as a reference for your ears.

Wednesday
February
28

2007

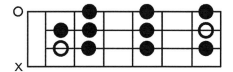

The frequency of "A" above middle C is 440 cycles (vibrations) per second.

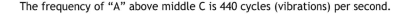

Note-A-Day
Calendars

Saturday
November
3
2007

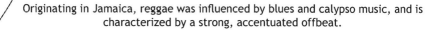

Today, play everything as loudly as possible.

Originating in Jamaica, reggae was influenced by blues and calypso music, and is characterized by a strong, accentuated offbeat.

Note-A-Day
Calendars

Thursday
March

1

2007

Taking one "fret" at a time, name all of the notes
on the 3rd, 5th, 7th, and 9th "frets", starting from
the fourth string and moving towards the first (e.g.,
for the open strings, it would be C, G, D, A).

Review your musical goals today.

Friday
November
2
2007

Play the following major scale.

Play it again, singing each note as you play it - use the syllables do (1), re (2), mi (3), fa (4), sol (5), la (6), ti (7), do (8), with each syllable corresponding to the note in the scale.

Next, play the root (first) note. Sing the second note (using re), then play the third note. Sing the fourth note (using fa), play the fifth, etc., ascending and descending.

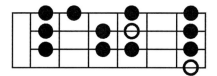

A Diamond Record, created in 1998, is the award given to a performing artist (typically musical artist) for the sale of ten million units of records, CDs, or cassettes.

Note-A-Day
Calendars

Friday
March
2

2007

Always make sure your hands are warm before you play. Playing with cold hands can cause injury.

Some ways to warm your hands include using a fire/heater, putting them close to your skin, running them under hot water, shaking them and/or moving your body, rubbing them together or massaging them, or having someone else rub them.

Adrien-François Servais was a 19th Century Belgian cellist who, in his time, was considered by many to be the equal of Niccolo Paganini, the most famous violinist of any era.

Thursday
November

1

2007

Memorize how to spell the major pentatonic scale (1, 2, 3, 5, 6).

Memorize and play the Db major pentatonic scale on the fourth string only, then play it using the pattern below.

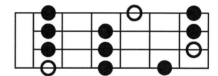

Review your musical goals today.

Saturday
March

3

2007

Practice bass-chord playing.

Play the progression C-F-G-C. Pluck the bass (lowest) note of the chord with your thumb, then play the rest of the chord, either strumming or plucking with your fingers.

Do this evenly, playing one bass note and one strum per click of the metronome). Gradually increase the tempo. You can also try this with your bow instead of your fingers.

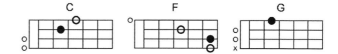

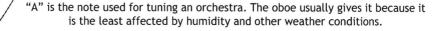

"A" is the note used for tuning an orchestra. The oboe usually gives it because it is the least affected by humidity and other weather conditions.

Note-A-Day
Calendars

Wednesday
October
31

2007

Play the major scale below.

Play it again, singing each note as you play it - use the syllables do (1), re (2), mi (3), fa (4), sol (5), la (6), ti (7), do (8), with each syllable corresponding to the note in the scale.

Next, play the root (first) note, then the second note. Sing them, using the syllables do and re. Play the root note, then the third note; sing them using do and mi. Play the root note, then the fourth note; sing them using do and fa. Continue doing this for the whole scale, ascending and descending.

Led Zeppelin's "Black Dog" was named because a huge black dog entered the studio when they were recording the song.

Sunday
March

4

2007

Memorize the following chord qualities:

eleventh (11) (1, 3, 5, 7, 11)
thirteenth (13) (1, 3, 5, 7, 13)

Spell each with A as the root (see the preface).

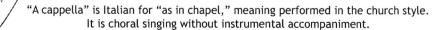

"A cappella" is Italian for "as in chapel," meaning performed in the church style.
It is choral singing without instrumental accompaniment.

Note-A-Day Calendars

Tuesday
October

30

2007

Choose a song played on a different instrument
and transcribe it by ear for cello.

"You build on failure. You use it as a stepping-stone. You don't try to forget the mistakes, but you don't dwell on it. You don't let it have any of your energy or any of your time, or any of your space." – Johnny Cash

Note-A-Day
Calendars

Monday
March

5

2007

Experiment with tuning your cello in fourths, like a guitar.

Tune the strings to C-F-Bb-Eb. Improvise, and see what sounds you create and new ideas you come up with.

Few symphonies are set in A minor, as it is considered the key of resignation.

Monday
October
29
2007

Make a date to go to a music store and play a similar instrument to the cello (i.e., stringed and having a fingerboard), such as a guitar, bass, dulcimer, mandolin, banjo, ukulele, etc. Notice the differences and similarities between it and the cello.

Motown is the term that refers to the style of music that emerged in Detroit, Michigan in the late 1960s. The "Motown Sound" was a mixture of several popular musical styles and can be considered a form of soul music.

Note-A-Day
Calendars

Tuesday
March
6
2007

Perform at least one song for young children (under 8 years old), either at a school or other similar setting. Don't choose anything that's too loud, or that you sense they wouldn't appreciate.

Tell them a little bit about the cello, such as how to play it, its different parts, etc.

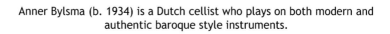

Anner Bylsma (b. 1934) is a Dutch cellist who plays on both modern and authentic baroque style instruments.

Sunday
October
28
2007

Memorize the notes in the chromatic scale:
A, A#/Bb, B, C, C#/Db, D, D#/Eb, E, F, F#/Gb, G, G#/Ab

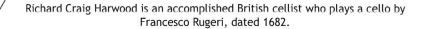

Richard Craig Harwood is an accomplished British cellist who plays a cello by
Francesco Rugeri, dated 1682.

Note-A-Day
Calendars

Wednesday
March
7

2007

Come up with your own creative idea today! Think of something you've never tried or done before and do it, or use something familiar that works well for you.

E-mail your idea to tips@Note-A-Day.com, and if we use it, we'll send you a free 2008 calendar!

"Please don't correct the wrong notes. The wrong notes are right." - composer Charles Ives to a copyist

Note-A-Day

Calendars

Saturday
October
27

2007

Choose a song with vocals and cello, and practice singing while playing the cello part.

Gutbucket is a style of jazz/blues playing first started by Louis Armstrong in "Gut Bucket Blues," ca. 1927. It became a popular style of jazz with early New Orleans and Chicago jazz musicians.

Note-A-Day
Calendars

Thursday
March
8
2007

Compose a song of any length or style. Memorize it.

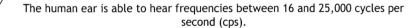

The human ear is able to hear frequencies between 16 and 25,000 cycles per second (cps).

Memorize the following chord qualities:

major (M) (1, 3, 5)
minor (m) (1, b3, 5)

Spell each with A as the root (see the preface).

Dolce means to play a passage sweetly, softly, and with tender emotion.

Practice the following major scale in this manner: ascending and descending in half-notes, then quarter-notes, then eighth-notes.

Next, start on the root and skip to the third note in the scale, back to the second note, skip to the fourth, etc., ascending and descending in all of the above rhythms.

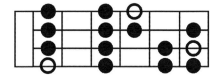

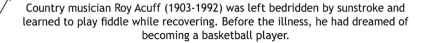

Country musician Roy Acuff (1903-1992) was left bedridden by sunstroke and learned to play fiddle while recovering. Before the illness, he had dreamed of becoming a basketball player.

<u>2008 Note-A-Day E-Calendars are here!</u>

Save a tree!

Never miss a lesson!

The Note-A-Day E-Calendars are a convenient, less-expensive alternative to the desktop calendars. They have all the same features, but without the paper or the size. Plus, you can search for lessons using the electronic index!

The E-Calendars are easy to install and customize. Choose when you want the lessons to pop-up on your screen. E-Calendars are available for all instruments!

To order, visit our website:
www.Note-A-Day.com/E-Calendars

Introducing the 2007 Note-A-Day E-Calendars

Save a tree!

Never miss a lesson!

The Note-A-Day E-Calendars are a convenient, less-expensive alternative to the desktop calendars. They have all the same features, but without the paper or the size. Plus, you can search for lessons using the electronic index!

The E-Calendars are easy to install and customize. Choose when you want the lessons to pop-up on your screen. E-Calendars are available for all instruments!

To order, visit our website:
www.Note-A-Day.com/E-Calendars

Order your 2008 calendar!

2008 calendars are here! They feature 366 lessons, including over 100 new lessons, new "factoids" and trivia, and more!

Indicate the quantity desired below:

....

__ 2008 Calendar for Bass   __ 2008 Calendar for Piano
__ 2008 Calendar for Cello   __ 2008 Calendar for Viola
__ 2008 Calendar for Double Bass   __ 2008 Calendar for Violin
__ 2008 Calendar for Guitar   __ 2008 Calendar for Voice

....

Shipping/handling:
(1-5) $2.95 each
(6-10) $1.95 each
(10+) $1.75 each

Total calendars ___ x $11.95 each = _____

Shipping/handling = _____

Total = _____

To order, enclose a copy of this form along with check or money order for the total amount and mail to:
Note-A-Day Calendars, PO Box 15167, Portland, OR 97293
To order using a credit card, go to www.Note-A-Day.com

Note-A-Day Calendars

Saturday
March
10

2007

Memorize one scale from the Circle of Fifths (see the preface).
Play it on one string, then play it using the pattern below.

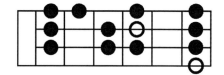

Although Justus Johann Friedrich Dotzauer wrote many symphonies, concertos, operas, and sonatas, he was most recognized for his "Violoncellschules," three volumes of 180 exercises and caprices for unaccompanied cello.

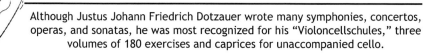

Note-A-Day
Calendars

Thursday
October

25

2007

It's been shown in different studies that teachers remember more information from their classes than their students!

One of the best ways to learn or practice something is to teach it. Teach someone something you know about or can play on the cello, and use it to build your confidence and share your knowledge.

"It's like a whole orchestra, the piano for me." - Dave Brubeck

Note-A-Day
Calendars

Sunday
March
11
2007

Choose a stringed instrument.

While practicing, improvising, or playing a song, imagine that you are playing that instrument instead of your cello. How would it sound and feel?

Try holding your cello as you would hold the instrument. Notice how it affects your playing.

The added-sixth chord (e.g., C, E, G, A) was first used by Claude Debussy and others in the early 20th century.

Wednesday
October
24

2007

Improvise with the minor pentatonic scale below, occasionally
playing notes that aren't in the scale.

Notice how these notes sound with the scale, how well
they do or don't fit, and which sounds you like.

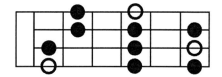

James Hesford, originally a jazz guitarist, formed Cellorhythmics (cello quartet
and percussion) with the leading classical cellist Alfia Nakipbekova (Bekova).

Monday
March
12

2007

Memorize barre chords for major and minor chords, using the fourth string as a root. Practice them in low and high positions, making sure each note rings clearly.

Major

Minor (m)

"Cannonball" Adderley, saxophonist and bandleader, got his nickname from a mispronunciation of "cannibal," in reference to his large appetite.

Practice writing the following symbols:
bass clef; sharp; flat; natural; double-sharp; double-flat

Tuesday
October

23

2007

The downbeat is the first beat of the measure. When played under the direction of a conductor, it is signified by the downward movement of the conductor's hand.

Note-A-Day
Calendars

Tuesday
March

13

2007

Play a Cm chord.

Improvise a melody over it with your voice, playing
the chord only when you can't hear it any longer.
Do this for at least several minutes.

Cm

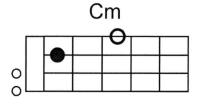

The treble clef is also known as the G clef.

Note-A-Day
Calendars

Monday
October
22
2007

Improvise slowly. Try to sing each note as you play it.
Don't worry whether you get it right or not - just do your
best. Notice how this affects your improvisation.

Baroque music is usually characterized by energetic, steady, and repetitive
rhythms.

Wednesday
March

14

2007

Tune your cello to "open G" tuning: B, G, D, G (low to high).

Experiment and improvise using this tuning. See
how quickly you can tune between this tuning
and standard tuning without using a tuner.

Oscar Pettiford is considered the pioneer of the cello as a solo instrument in jazz
music. In 1949, after suffering a broken arm, Pettiford found it impossible to
play his bass, so he experimented with a cello that a friend had lent him.

Play a song you either have memorized or can read through from start to finish.

Play it as slowly as possible (don't worry about mistakes). Next, play it as quickly as possible. Then, play it as restrained as possible, then as wild as possible.

Now, play it normally. Is it easier and/or different to play? You may arrive at choices that you'd like to use in performance.

Sunday
October
21

2007

The dominant chord is the chord or triad that is based on the fifth tone of a scale. In the key of C, the dominant triad is G.

Thursday
March

15

2007

Play the following chord progression in different musical genres, using different techniques.

C - F - G - C

Try different playing patterns, rhythms, tempos, arpeggios, etc. Some styles to try are rock, blues, reggae, funk, and jazz.

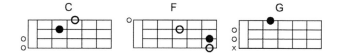

The bass clef is also known as the F clef.

Memorize one scale from the Circle of Fifths (see the preface).
Play it on one string, then using the pattern below.

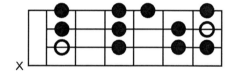

One of cellist Mark Summer's more unusual feats was playing a cello made of ice
on Taos Mountain at 11,000 feet.

Note-A-Day
Calendars

Friday
March
16

2007

Without looking at your cello, name all of the strings and "frets" where the following notes are found (e.g., Db is 4th string-1st "fret", 3rd string-6th "fret", etc.):
G#, C#, Db, A

Set your metronome to 60 bpm. Starting from the fourth string and moving one string at a time to the first, say which "fret" the note appears on with each click.

The fastest tempo mark is prestissimo (very rapid).

Note-A-Day
Calendars

Friday
October

19

2007

Memorize the following chord qualities:

augmented (aug or +) (1, 3, #5)
diminished (dim or °) (1, b3, b5)

Spell each with A as the root (see the preface).

"I'm saying: to be continued, until we meet again. Meanwhile, keep on listening and tapping your feet." - Count Basie

Note-A-Day
Calendars

Saturday
March

17

2007

Today, play everything as softly as possible.

Mezzo, as in mezzo piano, means "moderately."

Thursday
October
18

2007

Notice how your cello sounds in different rooms and spaces.
Try playing it in rooms such as a kitchen, bathroom, hallway,
bedroom, outside, etc.

Pay attention to the acoustics, noticing the effect they have
on your sound, and how that in turn affects your playing.

The primary movements of a Baroque suite are the allemande, courente,
sarabande, and gigue. Other optional movements include the prelude, menuet,
gavotte, air, bourée, and polonaise.

Note-A-Day Calendars

Sunday
March
18
2007

Memorize one scale from the Circle of Fifths (see the preface).
Play it on one string, then play it using the pattern below.

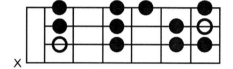

X

One reviewer wrote of Gretta Cohn, a cellist formerly of the group Cursive: "As
if ripping out the guts of an album, Cohn does not joke around with pretty string
chords, but goes after the music as if possessed by the essence of Slayer."

Note-A-Day
Calendars

Wednesday
October

17

2007

Put on a recording of a song that you know well and play a counter-melody or harmony to it. There are no wrong notes; if you play something that doesn't sound right, try a different note.

When reading sheet music, it is best to keep the music as close to eye-level as possible.

Note-A-Day
Calendars

Monday
March
19

2007

Play each of the following chords as an arpeggio (one note at a time, in order):

major ninth (maj9) (1, 3, 5, 7, 9)
minor ninth (m9) (1, b3, 5, b7, 9)

Play each with D as the root (see the preface).
Pay attention to the sound of each arpeggio.

A decrescendo is sometimes called a diminuendo.

Note-A-Day
Calendars

Tuesday
October
16
2007

If you normally sit while practicing, stand. If you normally stand, sit. Notice how this affects your playing.

Arthur Russell was an American cellist, composer, singer, and disco artist. Classically trained on the cello, he collaborated frequently with Allen Ginsberg in performance.

Note-A-Day
Calendars

Tuesday
March
20

2007

Memorize the following chord qualities and symbols:

half-diminished or minor seventh flat five (m7b5) (1, b3, b5, b7)
diminished seventh (dim7 or °7) (1, b3, b5, bb7)

Spell each with A as the root (see the preface).

A composer may increase or decrease the number of "f"s or "p"s in regard to
volume, e.g., fff, extremely loud, or pppppp, very, very soft.

Note-A-Day Calendars

Monday
October
15

2007

Memorize one scale from the Circle of Fifths (see the preface).
Play it on one string, then using the pattern below.

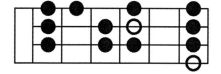

Rap, slang for conversation, was created by African-Americans in the mid 1970s.
It features rhyming lyrics that are often improvised and chanted to musical
accompaniment, which is often sampled from well-known songs.

Note-A-Day
Calendars

Wednesday
March
21
2007

Perform in front of a mirror. How do you look? Relaxed? Excited? Uncomfortable?

Make faces and/or change positions, and notice how doing so affects how you feel and how you play.

"Poco a poco" means "little by little."

Many musicians say that you need to be able to hear something
in your head before you can play it.

Choose a challenging musical passage and notice if you can hear
it clearly before you play it. If not, listen to a recording of it several
times, then try to hear it without the music.

If you don't have a recording of it, play the passage
very slowly, until you can imagine what it would
sound like when played at normal speed.

Sunday
October

14

2007

Equal temperament, the modern tuning system, involves tuning the octave
exactly, then dividing the octave into 12 equal semitones. In this system, thirds
are slightly under pitch.

Record yourself playing the major scale below, ascending only (give four counts before starting, using your voice).

Play back the recording. As it's playing, play the major scale again, only one half-step higher. Notice the harmony - it's probably not very soothing!

Continue playing back the recording and playing the pattern over it, moving the pattern one half-step higher each time. Listen to the different harmonies that are created.

Thursday
March
22

2007

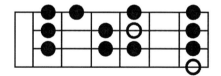

The word cello is short for violoncello, Italian for "little violone," now an obsolete instrument.

Note-A-Day
Calendars

Saturday
October
13

2007

Choose a note. Play it as softly as possible, gradually (slowly!)
increasing the volume with your right hand until you are playing it
as loudly as possible (crescendo).

Continue playing, gradually decreasing the volume
(decrescendo).

Notice the range available. Now play something familiar
(a riff or piece of music) at five different volumes.

"Beethoven can write music, thank God, but he can do nothing else on earth."
- Ludwig van Beethoven

Note-A-Day
Calendars

Friday
March
23

2007

Listen to a song and clap the beat with your hands
(you can also tap on your leg or a table). See if
you can stay on the beat for the entire song.

Calando, deficiendo, mancando, morendo, sminuendo, and smorzando are all
terms that mean, "growing slower and softer."

Note-A-Day
Calendars

Friday
October
12

2007

Whenever possible, use a metronome to help you stay "in time."
Keeping good time is essential, regardless of what you are
playing.

Always listen closely to the metronome, making
sure that the notes are landing exactly on the clicks.
Start slowly, gradually increasing speed after you
can play something perfectly at a slow speed.

The cello is a concert-pitched instrument.

Note-A-Day
Calendars

Saturday
March
24

2007

Memorize and learn to play one new chord today.

Use the preface, or visit http://4stringchords.com.

A chord is formed by a succession of three to five different tones.

Thursday
October

11

2007

If you have a standard practice routine, do something
different today; mix up the order, work on things you don't
typically practice, change your environment, etc.

8va (abbreviation for "at the octave") on a staff means to play one octave higher
than written. 8vb means to play one octave lower than written.

Play an "Ab". Improvise using the Ab Ionian mode for several minutes.

Occasionally play "Ab" or an Ab arpeggio as a reference for your ears.

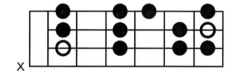

A three-tone chord is called a triad.

Note-A-Day
Calendars

Wednesday
October
10
2007

Taking one "fret" at a time, name all of the notes on the 1st, 3rd, 5th, 7th, and 9th "frets", starting from the fourth string and moving towards the first (e.g., for the open strings, it would be C, G, D, A).

A sonata consists of five forms or sections: introduction, exposition, development, recapitulation, and coda, with the introduction and coda being optional.

Note-A-Day
Calendars

Monday
March
26

2007

Tune your cello to "open A" tuning: C#, A, E, A (low to high).

Experiment and improvise using this tuning. See how quickly you can tune between this tuning and standard tuning without using a tuner.

Among the most famous Baroque works for cello are J.S. Bach's Unaccompanied Suites for Cello, or Bach Cello Suites.

Tuesday
October
9

2007

Practice artificial harmonics. Finger a note with your index finger, and lightly touch the string 2-1/2 steps above the note with your pinky. Bow close to the bridge; you should get a high-pitched overtone when done correctly. This may take some practice.

Experiment with different harmonics by increasing or decreasing the distance between your index finger and pinky.

An etude is a study or exercise designed to train a musician technically as well as musically.

Note-A-Day
Calendars

Tuesday
March
27

2007

Play an entire piece with your fingers instead of a bow. Be creative in making adjustments to compensate for this different technique.

A chord is called inverted when its root isn't the lowest tone.

Practice the following Phrygian mode pattern in this manner: ascending and descending in half-notes, then quarter-notes, then eighth-notes.

Next, start on the root and skip to the third note in the scale, back to the second note, skip to the fourth, etc., ascending and descending in all of the above rhythms.

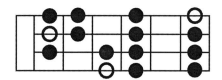

The cello is tuned C-D-G-A, one octave below the viola.

Note-A-Day
Calendars

Wednesday
March

28

2007

Play a D diminished chord.

Improvise a melody over it with your voice, playing
the chord only when you can't hear it any longer.
Do this for at least several minutes.

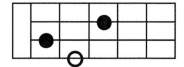

The Aeolian harp or lyre is a stringed instrument sounded by the wind.

Note-A-Day
Calendars

Sunday
October

7

2007

Research proper ways to clean and care for your cello, both the neck and the body. Clean it today.

A flag is the mark added to a note stem indicating the beat division of that note. Each flag added to any note will cut the duration of that note in half.

Note-A-Day
Calendars

Thursday
March
29

2007

Experiment with tones: try using guitar picks, different parts of the bow, different plucking techniques (using more or less nails, different angles, etc.), and different right-hand locations to create different tones.

Repeat the same musical idea each time to make it easier to compare the differences.

The theory that there is a relationship between music and human emotions is known as the Doctrine of Affects. It dates back to Greek antiquity, when the relationship was accepted as scientific fact.

Saturday
October
6
2007

If you can read music, put the page upside-down on the stand and play the music as it reads from the end. Play it with the same feeling as the original.

If you can't read music, try taking a familiar tune (such as Happy Birthday) and playing it backwards.

Notice how the music changes when played this way.

A fermata, or bird's eye, is a notation symbol indicating to sustain a note or chord indefinitely.

Friday
March

30

2007

Play each of the following chords as an arpeggio (one note at a time, in order):

add four (add4) (1, 3, 4, 5)
add nine (add9) (1, 3, 5, 9)

Play each with D as the root (see the preface).
Pay attention to the sound of each arpeggio.

The cello rests on a metal spike called an endpin.

Practice the following minor pentatonic scale in
the following rhythms, ascending and descending:
whole-, half-, quarter-, and eighth-notes.

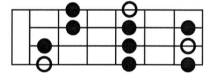

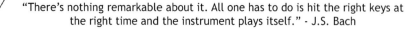

"There's nothing remarkable about it. All one has to do is hit the right keys at
the right time and the instrument plays itself." - J.S. Bach

Note-A-Day
Calendars

Saturday
March

31

2007

Play a piece of music you're familiar with. Notice how you are breathing throughout the entire piece (don't change it, just notice). Notice if and how your breath changes during specific parts. How does having this awareness affect your playing?

"If music be the food of love, play on." – The Duke of Illyria in Shakespeare's "Twelfth Night"

Note-A-Day
Calendars

Thursday
October
4
2007

Performing songs in public is often more difficult than practicing them by yourself. To compensate for this, practice your performance pieces faster than you'll actually perform them (once you have them mastered, not while learning them).

Today, take a song that you know well and practice it slightly faster than usual.

The sides (or ribs) of a cello are made by heating the wood and bending it around forms.

Note-A-Day
Calendars

Sunday
April
1

2007

Memorize the following chord qualities and symbols:

major sixth (6) (1, 3, 5, 6)
minor sixth (m6) (1, b3, 5, 6)

Spell each with A as the root (see the preface).

Review your musical goals today.

Note-A-Day
Calendars

Wednesday
October
3

2007

Visualizing is a convenient and powerful way to practice when you're away from your cello.

Choose a song that you're memorized, and visualize all of the left hand fingerings from start to finish.

Musicology is the study of music and its effect on society throughout the ages. It studies the music itself, the instruments used, the people who influenced the music, and the societies that produced it.

Monday
April
2

2007

Play one note and bow across all four strings. Move your finger up one half-step and play all four strings.

Continue moving it up one half-step at a time and playing. Listen to the different sounds you can get from this one "shape."

Traditionally, the cello has a spruce top with maple back, sides, and neck.

Put on a recording of a song that you can play well and dance to it.

Tuesday
October
2
2007

Scan through your body and move each part of it to the music. If you feel tension in any part, breathe deeply and relax that part. See if you can get lost in the music and quiet your mind.

Afterwards, play the song on the cello and notice how your playing has changed.

A virtuoso is someone who displays unusual or outstanding technique and ability in music.

Practice the G harmonic minor scale (1, 2, b3, 4, 5, b6, 7) in this manner: ascending and descending in half-notes, then quarter-notes, then eighth-notes.

Next, start on the root and skip to the third note in the scale, back to the second note, skip to the fourth, etc., ascending and descending in all of the above rhythms.

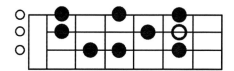

Ab major is considered a key of joy and celebration.

Note-A-Day
Calendars

Monday
October
1

2007

Break down areas of practice into smaller categories.

Instead of just practicing scales, divide into types of scales, keys, patterns, rhythms, etc.

Instead of just learning a song, break it down into researching the song, practicing the rhythms, isolating difficult parts, learning the theory, etc.

Setting smaller goals make them easier to reach and less overwhelming, and provides more motivation to continue.

Review your musical goals today.

Play a major scale. While playing the scale, sing the note that is four notes below the one you are playing (while staying in the scale). Tip: first play the note you'll be singing to learn the pitch, then go back and play the first note while singing the second one.

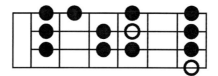

Polyrhythm is when two or more rhythms are played at the same time.

Without looking at your cello, name all of the strings and "frets" where the following notes are found (e.g., Db is 4th string-1st "fret", 3rd string-6th "fret", etc.):
A#, C, E, Gb

Set your metronome to 60 bpm. Starting from the fourth string and moving one string at a time to the first, say which "fret" the note appears on with each click.

Do this separately with each of the notes above.

Sunday
September
30

2007

The neck, pegbox, and scroll are normally carved from one piece of wood.

Note-A-Day
Calendars

Thursday
April
5

2007

Five minutes a day of focused practice yields better results than 15 minutes of unfocused practice. And, five minutes a day is more than not practicing at all.

Focus on the quality of your practice time, not the quantity. Five minutes a day adds up to over 30 hours a year!

Microtones are notes that fall between the steps of the chromatic scale.

Musicians often accumulate tension in their bodies over time. To avoid injury and achieve optimum results, regularly give yourself a massage to relax and loosen up your muscles.

Saturday
September
29

2007

Start with your shoulders and work your way down to your hands. Use as much pressure as feels good to you, going as deep as possible. If there are any tense areas, focus on them longer. (If possible, ask someone else to massage you, or get a professional massage. Also have them work on your chest and back).

Wunderkind is synonymous with prodigy, someone who displays great skill at an early age.

Friday
April
6

2007

Memorize barre chords for major seventh and minor seventh chords, using the fourth string as a root. Practice them in low and high positions, making sure each note rings clearly.

Major 7 (maj7)

Minor 7 (m7)

The cello is a descendant of the bass violin, first used by Claudio Monteverdi, which was a three-stringed instrument.

Note-A-Day
Calendars

Friday
September
28

2007

Restring your cello using a brand and/or gauge
of strings that you've never tried before.

"I just wanted a song to sing, and there came a point where I couldn't sing
anything . . . nobody else was writing what I wanted to sing. I couldn't find it
anywhere. If I could I probably would never have started writing." – Bob Dylan

Practice extending your reach with your left hand: put your index finger on the A string, 5th "fret" (D). Pluck, then put your middle finger on the 6th "fret" (D#) and play while holding your index finger down. Repeat, except this time put your middle finger on the 7th "fret" (E). Repeat again, putting it on the 8th "fret" (F).

DO THIS SLOWLY AND GENTLY! Do not force yourself to stretch-if you feel any pain, stop immediately. The goal is to stretch, not injure yourself.

Holding the index finger down, do this with each finger (index-ring, index-pinky), only stretching as far as comfortable. Repeat, middle-ring, middle-pinky. Repeat again with ring-pinky.

Warm up for this by pulling on and massaging each finger for a minute or two.

Saturday
April
7

2007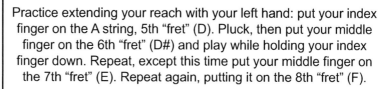

"Air on the G String" is the nickname of the air from J.S. Bach's "Orchestral Suite No. 3."

Note-A-Day
Calendars

Thursday
September
27

2007

Improvise using only double stops (two notes
played simultaneously, on either adjacent
strings, or separated by one string).

A waltz is in 3/4 time.

Note-A-Day
Calendars

Sunday
April

8

2007

Find a great local teacher and take a lesson from him or her (you can ask at a music store for recommendations).

Palm wine is a light and ethereal style originally played on acoustic guitar. It is accompanied by traditional percussion instruments. It gets its name from a sweet brew drunk in the bars and dance halls of Sierra Leone.

Note-A-Day
Calendars

Wednesday
September
26
2007

Experiment with creating your own chords.

Take a C major scale (C, D, E, F, G, A, B) and choose three notes. Play those three notes together to create chord. Listen carefully to the sound.

Create four more chords using this method. Use this method to come up with new sounds. You can do this with any scale.

The cello developed with the advent of wire-wound strings by Bolognese makers around 1660.

Note-A-Day Calendars

Monday
April
9

2007

Play an "Ab". Improvise using the Ab Locrian mode for several minutes.

Occasionally play "Ab" or an Ab diminished arpeggio as a reference for your ears.

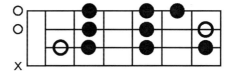

Aleatory music (Latin, alea, a dice game) is music composed or played by chance, using some random method of deciding which notes to play.

Tuesday
September
25

2007

Play a piece of music for someone. After you finish, ask
the person what they liked and didn't like about the piece
and how you played it. Use their feedback to improve.

Melomania is a great passion, or excessive or abnormal attraction to, music.

Note-A-Day
Calendars

Tuesday
April

10

2007

Play the major scale below, ascending and descending, playing each note twice in a row. Do this in quarter-notes, then eighth-notes.

When you feel comfortable with this, play each note three times in a row using quarter-notes, then eighth-notes.

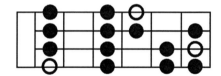

Italians popularized the cello in northern Europe around 1700.

Monday
September
24

2007

Play a note while positioning your right hand over the high end of the fingerboard.

Play the note several times, each time gradually moving the bow towards the bridge. Notice the tone in each position.

Play a piece of music you're familiar with five times, each time with your playing hand in a different position.

The Gothic period refers to the period of music in the late middle ages (A.D. 1100-1450).

Note-A-Day
Calendars

Wednesday
April

11

2007

Pick a date to go watch an accomplished cellist perform.
Some places to check for upcoming concerts include local
newspapers, college campuses, coffeehouses, music stores,
the Internet, and nearby stadiums, arenas, or recital halls.

Composer Irving Berlin never learned to formally read or write music.

Note-A-Day
Calendars

Sunday
September
23
2007

Cello:
A four-stringed musical instrument of the violin family, pitched lower than the viola but higher than the double bass. It is held upright between a seated player's knees and played with a bow. The cello has a full deep sound.

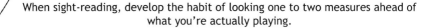

When sight-reading, develop the habit of looking one to two measures ahead of what you're actually playing.

Thursday
April
12

2007

Pay attention to your right hand today. Does it look or feel relaxed
or strained? Are you holding it at an awkward angle?

Keep your awareness on this hand today during everything
that you practice. Adjust and experiment with your hand and
wrist, striving for both a good tone and a relaxed position.

To alter a written note means to use an accidental to raise or lower the pitch of
the note.

When improvising over chords, the possibilities are endless. Here are two ideas you can use:

1. Play a different scale over each chord. If the chord is major, use a major scale (or mode). If it's minor, use a minor scale (or mode). Same for diminished, dominant, or augmented. Practice playing the scales in the same order as the chords, and for the same duration.

2. Play one scale over a group of chords. Write down all of the notes in the chords, and combine them to create and/or match up to a scale. Use this scale over the chords (you may have to leave out certain notes in the scale over certain chords if they don't sound good to you).

Saturday
September
22
2007

The cello is in the viola da braccio (viol of the arm) family, which includes the violin. It is not related to the viola da gamba, like the double bass.

Note-A-Day
Calendars

Friday
April
13

2007

Play the major scale below.

Play it again, singing each note as you play it - use the syllables do (1), re (2), mi (3), fa (4), sol (5), la (6), ti (7), do (8), with each syllable corresponding to the note in the scale.

Next, play the root (first) note. Sing that note, then sing (without playing) the entire scale, ascending and descending.

Anacrusis (Greek, upbeat) is the weak beat or weak part of a measure where a piece or phrase begins.

Note-A-Day
Calendars

Friday
September
21
2007

Play a major scale. While playing the scale, sing the note that is three notes below the one you are playing (while staying in the scale). Tip: first play the note you'll be singing to learn the pitch, then go back and play the first note while singing the second one.

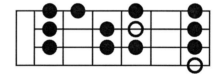

"I can't talk about my singing. I'm inside it. How can you talk about something you're inside of?" - Janis Joplin

Note-A-Day
Calendars

Saturday
April

14

2007

Taking one "fret" at a time, name all of the notes on the 2nd, 6th, 8th, and 10th "frets", starting from the fourth string and moving towards the first (e.g., for the open strings, it would be C, G, D, A).

Before endpins, cellos were supported by the player's calves. Before that, some players actually played them on the shoulder like a giant violin.

Note-A-Day
Calendars

Thursday
September
20
2007

Play a piece of music written for the violin on
the cello (transposing it down to pitch).

Heterophony is the practice of two or more musicians simultaneously performing
slightly different versions of the same melody.

Sunday
April

15

2007

Create your own pentatonic (five note) scale.
Improvise with it, and/or create a song.

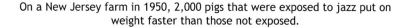

On a New Jersey farm in 1950, 2,000 pigs that were exposed to jazz put on
weight faster than those not exposed.

Note-A-Day
Calendars

Wednesday
September
19
2007

Look up and memorize definitions and/or notation for the following terms (www.8notes.com/glossary is a great resource):
crescendo, decrescendo, forte, pianissimo,
mezzo forte, mezzo piano

New age music is defined as music that is conducive to meditation. It is usually produced by layering sounds over sounds to produce a deep, multi-faceted wave of music.

Monday
April
16

2007

Practice the following minor pentatonic scale in the following rhythms, ascending and descending:
whole-, half-, quarter-, and eighth-notes.

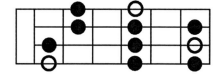

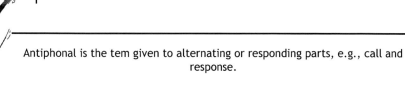

Antiphonal is the tem given to alternating or responding parts, e.g., call and response.

Note-A-Day
Calendars

Tuesday
September
18
2007

Memorize and learn to play one new chord today.

Use the preface, or visit http://4stringchords.com.

Many say that, of all the instruments, the cello's sound most resembles the human voice.

Learn and experiment with the Piongio scale:
1, 2, 4, 5, 6, b7

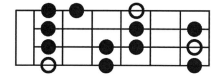

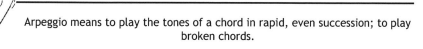

Arpeggio means to play the tones of a chord in rapid, even succession; to play broken chords.

Note-A-Day Calendars

Monday
September
17

2007

Practice memorizing and playing the following intervals (an interval is the distance between two notes):

minor second (m2); ½-step or 1 "fret"; Example: G# to A
minor third (m3); 1-½ steps or 3 "frets"; Example: F to Ab

Play the higher note, then the lower note. Sing both. Play both notes simultaneously. Sing both. Memorize the sound.

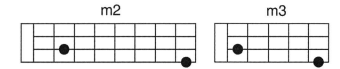

The Hyperaeolian mode is the mode starting on the seventh tone of the major scale (e.g., in the key of C, the Hyperaeolian mode starts on B). It is also called the Locrian mode.

Wednesday
April
18

2007

Practice memorizing and playing the following intervals (an interval is the distance between two notes):

perfect fourth (P4); 2-½ steps or 5 "frets"; Example: E to A
perfect fifth (P5); 3-½ steps or 7 "frets"; Example: E to B

Play the higher note, then the lower note. Sing both. Play both notes simultaneously. Sing both. Memorize the sound.

P4

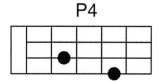

P5

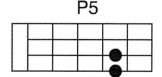

In early times, female cellists had to position the instrument to the side of both legs, since it was considered improper for a lady to spread her legs in public.

Play the following minor scale.

Play it again, singing each note as you play it - use the syllables do (1), re (2), mi (3), fa (4), sol (5), la (6), ti (7), do (8), with each syllable corresponding to the note in the scale.

Next, play the root (first) note, then the second note. Sing both, using syllables do and re. Play the root note, then the third note; sing both using do and mi. Play the root note and the fourth note; sing both using do and fa. Continue doing this for the whole scale, ascending and descending.

Sunday
September
16

2007

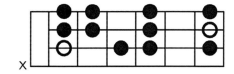

"If something is boring after two minutes, try it for four. If still boring, then eight. Then sixteen. Then thirty-two. Eventually one discovers that it is not boring at all." - John Cage

Practice the following major scale using alternate bowing (alternating up-bows and down-bows).

First play it starting with a down-bow, then play it starting with an up-bow.

Use a metronome, and play as quarter-notes, then eighth-notes.

Thursday
April
19
2007

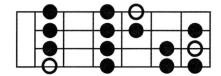

An arrangement is the adaptation of a composition for an instrument or collection of instruments for which it was not originally written.

Note-A-Day
Calendars

Saturday
September
15
2007

Create your own scale using any seven notes.
Improvise with it, and/or create a song.

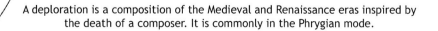

A deploration is a composition of the Medieval and Renaissance eras inspired by
the death of a composer. It is commonly in the Phrygian mode.

Friday
April
20

2007

Play each of the following chords as an arpeggio (one note at a time, in order):

dominant seventh or seventh (7 or dom7) (1, 3, 5, b7)
dominant ninth or ninth (9) (1, 3, 5, b7, 9)

Play each with D as the root (see the preface).
Pay attention to the sound of each arpeggio.

Artificial harmonics are harmonics produced on a stopped string rather than on an open string.

Friday
September
14

2007

Dress up today for practicing, and notice
how it affects your playing.

In music of the Romantic era, vibrato is used on almost every note. It is rarely
used in Baroque music.

Note-A-Day Calendars

Saturday
April
21

2007

Experiment with breathing differently as you play a familiar song.

Play it once breathing rapidly, once breathing slowly, and once breathing normally.

Notice how your breathing affects (and is affected by) your playing.

An augmented triad consists of two major thirds, as in C, E, G#.

Note-A-Day
Calendars

Thursday
September

13

2007

Learn and experiment with the Blues scale:
1, b3, 4, b5, 5, b7

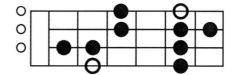

Improvisation refers to the spontaneous performance of music without previous
preparation or any written notes.

Practice memorizing and playing the following intervals (an interval is the distance between two notes).

major second (M2); 1 step or 2 "frets"; Example: Gb to Ab
major third (M3); 2 steps or 4 "frets"; Example: F to A

Play the higher note, then the lower note. Sing both. Play both notes simultaneously. Sing both. Memorize the sound.

Sunday
April
22
2007

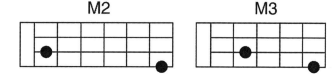

The place where you grip a bow is called the frog.

Note-A-Day
Calendars

Wednesday
September

12

2007

Think of one or two people who you know well. Improvise, mimicking their voice and manner of speaking (don't do this if they are around, unless you have their permission).

"I don't have enough hair to be a genius." - Beck

Monday
April
23
2007

Play the shape below (octave).

Move the shape up one half-step and play again. Continue moving the shape up one half-step and playing it until you reach the 10th "fret", then back down again to the first "fret".

Repeat, playing two "frets" per click of the metronome (eighth-notes).

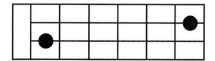

Johann Sebastian Bach had 20 children, 10 of which reached maturity.

Tuesday
September

11

2007

Experiment with different ways of playing chords. Some ideas include:

• Bowing down vs. bowing up
• Playing notes individually (arpeggios)
• Sliding into the chord by holding the shape one half-step above or below the desired location and sliding to the actual pitch that you want
• Holding a chord and using vibrato on it
• Playing with fingers instead of the bow
• Playing the lowest (bass note) of the chord then playing the upper notes

Create your own techniques in addition to these.
Choose one chord with which to experiment.

A "lick" refers to a short phrase or series of notes.

Note-A-Day
Calendars

Tuesday
April
24

2007

The ii-V-I chord progression is very common in jazz. Learn to recognize the sound of it.

Two progressions to practice with are Am-D-G and Dm-G-C.

There are 12 tones used in most music, although microtones are increasing in usage.

Memorize how to spell the three primary minor scales:

- Natural minor (1, 2, b3, 4, 5, b6, b7)
- Harmonic minor (1, 2, b3, 4, 5, b6, 7)
- Melodic minor (1, 2, b3, 4, 5, 6, 7)

Spell each with A as the root.

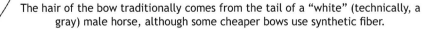

The hair of the bow traditionally comes from the tail of a "white" (technically, a gray) male horse, although some cheaper bows use synthetic fiber.

Note-A-Day
Calendars

Wednesday
April
25

2007

Practice the right-hand parts to a song of your choice, playing them without the left hand.

The piano was originally called the piano-forte (soft-loud). It was named for its ability to play at different volumes, unlike its predecessor, the harpsichord.

Note-A-Day
Calendars

Sunday
September
9

2007

Learn and experiment with the Ethiopian scale:
1, 2, b3, 4, 5, b6, b7

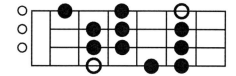

A cent is a unit of measure for musical intervals. 1200 cents equal one octave.

Note-A-Day
Calendars

Thursday
April
26
2007

Notice any limiting ideas and beliefs you have about your cello-related abilities or desires. Some examples include "I'm not as good as so and so," "I started playing too late in life to be any good," "I'm not a natural musician," "I can't make a living making music," etc.

Write them down. Read through the list. Before each one, say, "I'm choosing to let go of this belief."

Then, crumple up, shred, and/or flush or throw away the paper. Repeat this practice regularly.

Double stopping is when two separate strings are stopped by the fingers and bowed simultaneously, producing part of a chord.

Note-A-Day
Calendars

Below is a list of the seven modes created from the major scale, as well as the chords they work best with:

Ionian (Major)
Dorian (minor)
Phrygian (minor)
Lydian (Major)
Mixolydian (Major or Dominant)
Aeolian (minor)
Locrian (diminished)

Saturday
September
8

2007

The Romantic Era is the musical period from about 1800-1900. It is characterized by an emphasis on emotional qualities, freedom of form, increased use of chromaticism, and expanded tonality.

Note-A-Day
Calendars

Friday
April
27

2007

Record your entire practice session today.

Listen back to it, and notice both positive areas and areas where you can improve. Some things to notice are the quality of what you played (sloppy vs. clean), how musical you were, if you played "in time," if you rushed through anything, if certain areas could use more time, etc.

The order of sharps in the Circle of Fifths is the reverse of the flats: F#, C#, G#, D#, A#, E#, B#.

Note-A-Day
Calendars

Friday
September
7

2007

Practice alternate bowing between the open C and D strings.
Alternate between them in four measures each of whole-
notes, half-notes, quarter-notes, and eighth-notes. Then
consecutively play one measure of each of the above rhythms.

"If we were all determined to play the first violin we should never have an
ensemble." – Robert Schumann

Note-A-Day
Calendars

Saturday
April

28

2007

Memorize and learn to play one new chord today.

Use the preface, or visit http://4stringchords.com.

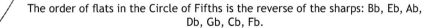

The order of flats in the Circle of Fifths is the reverse of the sharps: Bb, Eb, Ab, Db, Gb, Cb, Fb.

Choose a song that you have memorized and that is challenging for you to play. Lay or sit in relaxed position and close your eyes. Imagine yourself playing the song.

As you imagine, pay attention to your body. Do you tense up or change your breathing at any point during the song?

Thursday
September
6

If so, isolate that part of the song. See if you can relax any tense body parts and maintain deep, even breathing as you imagine playing that part. It may take numerous times before you can do it easily - take your time.

2007

When you've got it, pick up your cello and play the song.

Vibrato is a poor substitute for good intonation, and will do little to cover up an out-of-tune note.

Note-A-Day
Calendars

Sunday
April
29

2007

Tune your cello to "open D" tuning: D, F#, D, A (low to high).

Experiment and improvise using this tuning. See
how quickly you can tune between this tuning
and standard tuning without using a tuner.

The singing of the syllables do, re, mi, etc. is called solfege.

Note-A-Day Calendars

Wednesday
September

5

2007

Play a Dm chord. First ascending, then descending, play each note of the chord and sing it, saying the syllable "la" (changing octaves as needed).

Play and sing the lowest note of the chord, then sing (without playing, ascending then descending) the rest of the notes.

Do this for Gm and Cm chords as well.

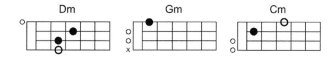

Dm   Gm   Cm

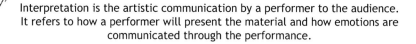

Interpretation is the artistic communication by a performer to the audience. It refers to how a performer will present the material and how emotions are communicated through the performance.

Note-A-Day
Calendars

Monday
April

30

2007

Improvise using only the ring finger on your left
hand (use your right hand as usual).

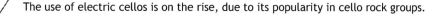

The use of electric cellos is on the rise, due to its popularity in cello rock groups.

Play a major scale. While playing the scale, sing the note that is five notes below the one you are playing (while staying in the scale). Tip: first play the note you'll be singing to learn the pitch, then go back and play the first note while singing the second one.

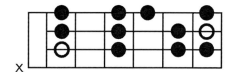

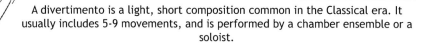

A divertimento is a light, short composition common in the Classical era. It usually includes 5-9 movements, and is performed by a chamber ensemble or a soloist.

Tuesday
May
1

2007

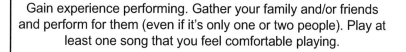

Gain experience performing. Gather your family and/or friends and perform for them (even if it's only one or two people). Play at least one song that you feel comfortable playing.

Before playing, talk briefly about what you're going to play. When you are completely finished, thank and acknowledge your audience.

Review your musical goals today.

Note-A-Day
Calendars

Monday
September

3

2007

Improvise, playing the second and fourth strings
simultaneously (play the second string with your index or
middle finger and the fourth string with your thumb).

Inflection is any change or modification of pitch or tone.

Note-A-Day
Calendars

Wednesday
May
2

2007

Improvise using "drones":

Finger notes only on the second (D) string while
playing the fourth, third, and second strings.
Use whatever scales and notes you like.

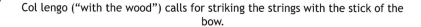

Col lengo ("with the wood") calls for striking the strings with the stick of the
bow.

Choose a major scale (use the pattern below). While playing
the scale, sing the note that is one note below the one
you are playing (while staying in the scale). Tip: first play
the note you'll be singing to learn the pitch, then go back
and play the first note while singing the second one.

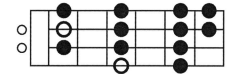

Attaching a mute (a small device made of metal or rubber) gives a more mellow
tone, with fewer audible overtones.

Thursday
May
3

2007

Memorize the following chord qualities:

dominant seventh or seventh (7 or dom7) (1, 3, 5, b7)
dominant ninth or ninth (9) (1, 3, 5, b7, 9)

Spell each with A as the root (see the preface).

A mode uses the notes of a scale, but begins on a note other than the keynote.

Note-A-Day
Calendars

Saturday
September

1

2007

Improvise using only your pinky on your left
hand (use your right hand as usual).

Review your musical goals today.

Note-A-Day
Calendars

Friday
May

4

2007

Improvise using no structure at all; don't use any particular scales, notes, chords, rhythms, styles, etc. See what you can create.

The difference between the major scale and the harmonic minor scale is the flat 3rd and 6th of the latter.

Note-A-Day
Calendars

Friday
August
31

2007

Eating habits affect your playing, including your energy level and ability to focus. Pay attention to the kinds of food you eat and how they affect your health and energy.

Notice how eating before you play or practice affects your energy and concentration, and how they change in response to the foods that you are eating. Wait at least one hour to practice after eating so that your body won't be using energy to digest the food.

An introduction is a preparatory movement, usually in a slow tempo, used to introduce a larger composition. The term is chiefly applied to Classical and Romantic music, but is not exclusively applicable to those eras.

Note-A-Day
Calendars

Saturday
May
5
2007

Improvise using only staccato (don't let notes ring for very long, don't use slides or long bowing strokes, use pizzicato).

While rehearsing, sit or stand in the position in which you will perform.

Thursday
August
30
2007

Go busking!

Choose a busy spot on a sidewalk, put out your cello case, and start playing. See if anyone throws some money your way (hint: put some bills and coins in the case before you start playing).

Chopping is a technique that involves striking the strings with the hair near the bottom of the bow. It is most commonly used by jazz musicians.

Sunday
May
6

2007

Choose a note. Make a facial expression and play the note in a
way that reflects to the facial expression.

Try this with different expressions (sad, happy, angry,
silly, etc.). Notice how this affects how you feel and
how you play. Experiment with entire songs.

Playing with the bow is called arco and plucking with fingers is called pizzicato.

Note-A-Day
Calendars

Wednesday
August
29

2007

Play each of the following chords as an arpeggio (one note at a time, in order):

suspended second or "sus two" (sus2) (1, 2, 5)
suspended fourth or "sus four" (sus4) (1, 4, 5)

Play each with D as the root (see the preface).
Pay attention to the sound of each arpeggio.

"I haven't understood a bar of music in my life, but I have felt it." - Igor Stravinsky

Monday
May
7

2007

Learn and experiment with the Hawaiian scale:
1, 2, b3, 4, 5, 6, 7

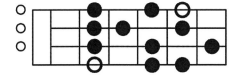

Death metal is a sub-genre of heavy metal featuring lyrics praising death. It uses rhythmic, chromatic progressions, and an ongoing development of themes and motifs, rather than a verse-chorus structure.

Memorize how to spell the diminished scale (1, b2, b3, 3, b5, 5, 6, b7).

Memorize and play the D diminished scale on the fourth string only, then play it using the pattern below.

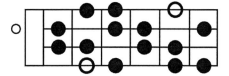

Tuesday
August
28
2007

Sub-genres of heavy metal music include thrash, speed, hardcore, grindcore, screamo, nü, rap, death, black, goth, glam, hair, pop, metalcore, and just plain metal, among others.

Practice the following Mixolydian mode pattern in this manner: ascending and descending in half-notes, then quarter-notes, then eighth-notes.

Next, start on the root and skip to the third note in the scale, back to the second note, skip to the fourth, etc., ascending and descending in all of the above rhythms.

Tuesday
May
8
2007

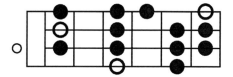

The intervals of the major scale ascend in this pattern: whole step-whole step-half-whole-whole-whole-half (W-W-H-W-W-W-H).

Note-A-Day
Calendars

Monday
August
27

2007

Repeating musical ideas makes whatever you play more
memorable and catchy.

Choose any scale and improvise. Create a phrase
or idea, and continue to come back to it, playing it
every few measures or so. Notice how this provides
a thread running through your improvisation.

A diminished chord is a chord that has a diminished interval between its highest
and lowest notes.

Wednesday
May
9

2007

Hold the bow upside-down (holding the head) and play that way today. See if you learn or discover anything new by doing this.

A dot increases the duration of a note by its original value plus ½.

Note-A-Day

Calendars

Sunday

August

26

2007

Improvise without playing two notes in a row that fall on the same or adjacent strings (skip at least one string between each note).

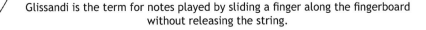

Glissandi is the term for notes played by sliding a finger along the fingerboard without releasing the string.

Note-A-Day
Calendars

Thursday
May
10
2007

Practice the following Dorian mode pattern in this manner: ascending and descending in half-notes, then quarter-notes, then eighth-notes.

Next, start on the root and skip to the third note in the scale, back to the second note, skip to the fourth, etc., ascending and descending in all of the above rhythms.

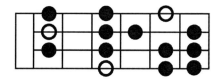

Spiccato is the term used for striking the strings with the bow, while still maintaining a horizontal motion. This produces a percussive, crisp sound.

Saturday
August
25

2007

Being relaxed will help you play better with less effort and avoid injury.

As you practice today, pause every few minutes to scan through your body (starting from your head and moving towards your feet). Take a full minute for each scan. Notice particular areas where you feel tense or tight, and areas where you feel relaxed.

Choose one tense body part, and focus your attention on it while taking deep breaths, using your breathing to release the tension.

Continue doing this with each tense area. Tension may return, so continue to scan your body and release any tension during your practice time.

"I'll play it and tell you what it is later." - Miles Davis

Practice the following Locrian mode pattern in this manner: ascending and descending in half-notes, then quarter-notes, then eighth-notes.

Next, start on the root and skip to the third note in the scale, back to the second note, skip to the fourth, etc., ascending and descending in all of the above rhythms.

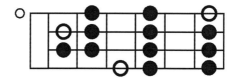

A march is in 4/4 time.

Practice the following Aeolian mode (minor scale) pattern in this manner: ascending and descending in half-notes, then quarter-notes, then eighth-notes.

Next, start on the root and skip to the third note in the scale, back to the second note, skip to the fourth, etc., ascending and descending in all of the above rhythms.

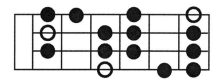

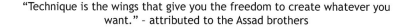

"Technique is the wings that give you the freedom to create whatever you want." - attributed to the Assad brothers

As you play or practice today, listen closely to the transition from every note or chord you play to the next note or chord.

How does this awareness affect your playing? Do you notice anything as you listen closely to these transitions?

To find the relative minor key of a major key, count one-and-a-half steps down from the root.

Note-A-Day
Calendars

Thursday
August
23
2007

Wear earplugs and headphones while you practice today, muffling your hearing as much as possible. Notice how this affects your playing.

When rehearsing a piece that you'll be performing, keep playing if you make a mistake.

Note-A-Day
Calendars

Sunday
May
13
2007

Play each of the following chords as an arpeggio (one note at a time, in order):

major sixth (6) (1, 3, 5, 6)
minor sixth (m6) (1, b3, 5, 6)

Play each with D as the root (see the preface).
Pay attention to the sound of each arpeggio.

Fine, pronounced fee-nay, is Italian for "the end."

Note-A-Day
Calendars

Wednesday
August

22

2007

Tune your cello to "open E" tuning: B, G#, E, G# (low to high).

Experiment and improvise using this tuning. See
how quickly you can tune between this tuning
and standard tuning without using a tuner.

Antonio Stradivari, famous for the Stradivarius violin, also made cellos, many of
which are still played today.

Monday
May

14

2007

Play the minor scale below.

Play it again, singing each note as you play it - use the syllables do (1), re (2), mi (3), fa (4), sol (5), la (6), ti (7), do (8), with each syllable corresponding to the note in the scale.

Next, play the root (first) note. Sing that note, then sing (without playing) the entire scale, ascending and descending.

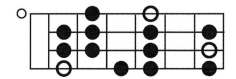

Orchestras usually include between eight and twelve cellists.

Note-A-Day
Calendars

Tuesday
August
21

2007

Research electronic pickups for amplifying cellos by typing
"amplify cello" into a search engine.

Learn how they work, how to use them, manufacturers,
and advantages or disadvantages to using them.

Maestro is a title of extreme respect given to a great performer, conductor,
instrument maker, or composer.

Note-A-Day
Calendars

Tuesday
May
15
2007

Practice writing the following notes:
whole-note; half-note; quarter-note; eighth-note; sixteenth-note
Write each at least five times.

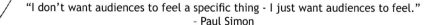

"I don't want audiences to feel a specific thing - I just want audiences to feel."
- Paul Simon

Note-A-Day
Calendars

Monday
August
20

2007

Memorize and learn to play one new chord today.

Use the preface, or visit http://4stringchords.com.

"In the end, I think of music as saving grace for all humanity." – Henry Miller

The essential components of music are tone (quality of sound or timbre, e.g., a trombone compared to a harp), pitch (how high or low a note is), rhythm (grouping and accentuation of notes), and dynamics (loud vs. soft).

Choose one note and experiment with
each of the four components.

Changes in the volume of a phrase are called dynamics.

Note-A-Day
Calendars

Sunday
August
19

2007

It's been said that music is the space between the notes. Today, pay particular attention to the space between all the notes that you play.

A cadenza is a solo in the midst of a concerto, often displaying virtuosic technique.

Thursday
May
17

2007

How often do you take breaks?

Ideally, take a break every 15-20 minutes. This will help you be more relaxed and focused when you return to practicing.

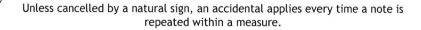

Unless cancelled by a natural sign, an accidental applies every time a note is repeated within a measure.

Note-A-Day
Calendars

Saturday
August

18

2007

As a warm-up exercise, practice the following finger patterns on one string on adjacent notes.

Choose one pattern at a time and play it at least four times in a row. Use a metronome, and play as sixteenth-notes (four notes per click of the metronome). Start slowly!

4-3-2-1
4-2-3-1
4-3-1-2
4-1-3-2

Edward Elgar hummed his cello concerto's opening theme to a friend during his final illness, telling him, "If even after I'm dead you hear someone whistling this tune on the Malvern Hills, don't be alarmed. It's only me."

Play a D chord. First ascending, then descending, play each note of the chord and sing it, saying the syllable "la" (changing octaves as needed).

Friday
May
18
2007

Play and sing the lowest note of the chord, then sing (without playing, ascending then descending) the rest of the notes.

Do this for C and C7 chords as well.

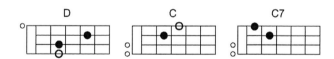

D   C   C7

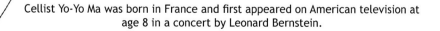

Cellist Yo-Yo Ma was born in France and first appeared on American television at age 8 in a concert by Leonard Bernstein.

Friday
August

17

2007

Choose a song with vocals. Figure out the vocal melody on the cello, and try to emulate the nuances of the voice by using slides, vibrato, bowing techniques, etc.

A nocturne is a composition, usually a serenade, which is meant to be played outside at night.

Note-A-Day
Calendars

Saturday
May
19

2007

Play a major scale in one octave. Play the first note loudly (forte).
Play the second note softly (piano).

Continue alternating in this way, both up and down the scale.
Play as quarter-notes, and gradually increase the tempo.

The term "band" traditionally refers to brass, woodwind, and percussion
instruments only, excluding the stringed instruments.

As you play your cello, pretend that you're playing another instrument (choose one). Does this change what or how you play?

Try holding your cello as you would that instrument. You can also experiment with techniques that pertain to that instrument, e.g., for piano, laying the cello flat and using your hands as you would on a piano.

A cadence brings a phrase to a more or less definite close.

Calendars

Sunday
May
20
2007

Choose a song you can play well. Play it at half
of its normal speed, using a metronome.

Another term for a guitar pick is a plectrum.

Wednesday
August
15

2007

Playing one note or chord (and using a metronome), play four measures of whole-notes (one note per four clicks in 4/4 time).

Next, play four measures of half-notes (one note per two clicks), four measures of quarter-notes (one note per click), four measures of eighth-notes (two notes per click), and four measures of sixteenth-notes (four notes per click), without pause.

Then, without pausing, reverse the order back to whole-notes.

After you can do this evenly and smoothly, play only one measure of each consecutively.

Eye music, most common in the Middle Ages and Renaissance eras, is music that may make no sense to the ear, but has a secret puzzle or message when visually analyzed.

Note-A-Day
Calendars

Monday
May
21

2007

Research the following cellists:
Aaron Minsky, Mark Summer, Adrien-François Servais, Mischa
Maisky, and Sarah Balliet.

See what you can learn about their styles
and contributions to the cello.

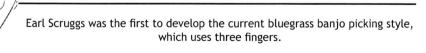

Earl Scruggs was the first to develop the current bluegrass banjo picking style,
which uses three fingers.

Tuesday
August
14

2007

Experiment with muting the strings while you play pizzicato.

Rest the heel of your right hand on the strings by the bridge and pluck the string that your hand is resting on.

Practice muting each string, adjusting the placement of your right hand as needed.

Fiddlestick is another word for the bow.

Practice the following Lydian mode pattern in this manner: ascending and descending in half-notes, then quarter-notes, then eighth-notes.

Next, start on the root and skip to the third note in the scale, back to the second note, skip to the fourth, etc., ascending and descending in all of the above rhythms.

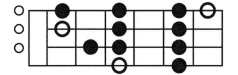

Tuesday
May
22
2007

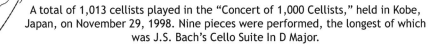

A total of 1,013 cellists played in the "Concert of 1,000 Cellists," held in Kobe, Japan, on November 29, 1998. Nine pieces were performed, the longest of which was J.S. Bach's Cello Suite In D Major.

Note-A-Day
Calendars

Using "p" on the fourth string, "i" on the 3rd string, "m" on the 2nd, and "a" on the 1st, play the following patterns several times each using a C or F chord:

Monday
August
13
2007

p, m, i, a
pima (simultaneously)
p, a, i, m
p, m, a, i

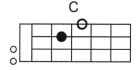

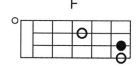

For sight-reading practice, never read through something more than once in a session, and never read the same music two days in a row.

Note-A-Day
Calendars

Wednesday
May
23
2007

Play the first letter of your name. Play it the same way as you would play a scale.

Next, play your whole name, starting each letter on any "fret" you like. Listen to the sounds, and notice what you do and don't like.

This shape would represent "A":

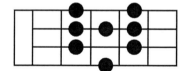

A bar or barline, first used in the 15th century, is a vertical line dividing measures on the staff.

Note-A-Day
Calendars

Sunday
August

12

2007

When performing, make sure that your stage setup is familiar and comfortable.

Plan enough time in advance to make sure that chairs and microphones are set to the proper height, that your equipment is accessible, and that you have everything you need such as extra strings, bows, rosin, water, etc.

If possible, take a few minutes before you perform to run through something you'll be playing and check that everything is set up properly.

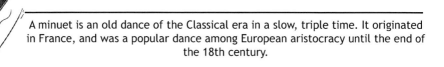

A minuet is an old dance of the Classical era in a slow, triple time. It originated in France, and was a popular dance among European aristocracy until the end of the 18th century.

Note-A-Day
Calendars

Thursday
May
24

2007

Practice vibrato (rapidly bending a string up and down or side-to-side) separately with each left-hand finger.

Experiment with different kinds of vibrato: wide vs. narrow, fast vs. slow. Practice in different positions on the neck.

Baroque music is the classical music developed between 1600 and 1750.

Note-A-Day
Calendars

Saturday
August
11

2007

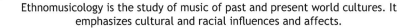

Choose a song you are learning or are interested in and research it. Research the composer, when the song was written, inspiration and/or meaning behind it, etc. Notice if this helps you feel more connected to the music.

Ethnomusicology is the study of music of past and present world cultures. It emphasizes cultural and racial influences and affects.

Look up and memorize definitions for the following music terms (www.8notes.com/glossary is a great resource): andante, presto, allegro, moderato, adagio

---

The word "baroque" is from the Portuguese "barroco," meaning an irregularly shaped pearl. It originally implied a bizarre, even crude, quality.

Play the chromatic scale pattern below, ascending (keeping previously-played fingers down on each string) and descending.

Using a metronome, play using quarter-notes, eighth-notes, and sixteenth-notes. Make each note as clear as possible, and make each note equal in volume and quality.

Gradually increase the tempo. This is a great warm-up exercise.

Friday
August
10

2007

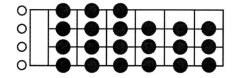

The world's largest orchestra consisted of 6,452 musicians from the Vancouver Symphony Orchestra and students throughout British Columbia. They played at BC Place Stadium, Vancouver, Canada, on May 15, 2000.

Saturday
May
26

2007

Take a piece of music that has both pizzicato and bowing and reverse the parts (play the pizzicato parts with the bow, the bowed parts with the fingers).

The oldest existing symphony orchestra, the Gewandhaus Orchestra of Leipzig, Germany, was established in 1743.

Note-A-Day
Calendars

Thursday
August

9

2007

Look up and memorize definitions for the following terms
(www.8notes.com/glossary is a good site to use):
mosso, poco, meno, a tempo, più

"The aim and final end of all music should be none other than the glory of God
and the refreshment of the soul." – J.S. Bach

Note-A-Day
Calendars

Sunday
May
27
2007

Improvise for five minutes using only one finger on your left hand.

A riff is a short, melodic, repeated musical phrase.

Practice the following minor pentatonic scale in
the following rhythms, ascending and descending:
whole-, half-, quarter-, and eighth-notes.

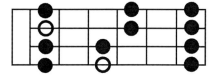

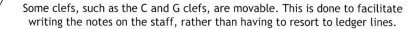

Some clefs, such as the C and G clefs, are movable. This is done to facilitate
writing the notes on the staff, rather than having to resort to ledger lines.

Practice memorizing and playing the following intervals (an interval is the distance between two notes).

major ninth (M9); 7 steps or 14 "frets"; Example: D to E (one octave above)
major thirteenth (M13); 10-½ steps or 21 "frets"; Example: D to B (one octave above)

Monday
May
28

2007

Play the higher note, then the lower note. Sing both. Play both notes simultaneously. Sing both. Memorize the sound.

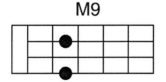

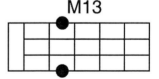

Klezmer music is derived from two Hebrew words, clay and zimmer, meaning "vessel of music."

Note-A-Day
Calendars

Tuesday
August
7

2007

Mute the strings on your cello with your left hand.

Improvise for five minutes while keeping the strings muted.
Experiment with playing one string, playing multiple strings,
playing different rhythms, playing close to or away from the
bridge, etc.

Pay particular attention to the rhythms. See how creative you
can be as you explore the percussive aspects of playing.

A fugue is a form of composition popular in, but not restricted to, the Baroque
era. In it, a theme or subject is introduced by one voice, and then is imitated by
other voices in succession.

Note-A-Day
Calendars

Tuesday
May
29
2007

Memorize and learn to play one new chord today.

Use the preface, or visit http://4stringchords.com.

The harmonica is the world's best-selling instrument.

Note-A-Day
Calendars

Monday
August
6

2007

Play the shape below (octave). Make sure the string in between the two notes is muted (silent). Move the shape up one half-step and play again.

Continue moving the shape up one half-step and playing it until you reach the tenth "fret", then back down again until you reach the first "fret".

Repeat, playing two "frets" per click of the metronome (eighth-notes).

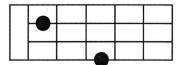

The cello is twice the size of the violin.

Note-A-Day Calendars

Play an "Ab". Improvise using the Ab Dorian mode for several minutes.

Occasionally play "Ab" or an Abm arpeggio as a reference for your ears.

Wednesday
May
30
2007

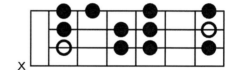

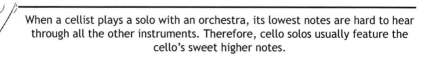

When a cellist plays a solo with an orchestra, its lowest notes are hard to hear through all the other instruments. Therefore, cello solos usually feature the cello's sweet higher notes.

Note-A-Day
Calendars

Sunday
August
5

2007

Find a piece of art that inspires you. Improvise, creating music that goes with the art.

"A great song is more than just words and music. It's a thumb pressing against the pulse of living that relates a simple truth about a very complicated process."
– Jimmy Buffett

Note-A-Day
Calendars

Thursday
May
31

2007

Listen to a style of music that you are not familiar with (go to www.Amazon.com or www.AllCoolMusic.com if you need to search for songs).

Notice the different instruments, what makes the style different from something you'd normally listen to, and how the music makes you feel. See if you can remain open and curious as you listen to it, and if you can learn or discover anything new.

The CD was developed by Philips and Sony in 1980.

Memorize how to spell the whole-tone scale (1, 2, 3, #4, #5, #6).

Memorize and play the scale only on the fourth string starting on Db, then using the pattern below.

Saturday
August
4

2007

Iscathamiya is Zulu call-and-response, a cappella choral music sung by men from South Africa.

Friday
June
1

2007

Learn and experiment with the Overtone scale:
1, 2, 3, #4, 5, 6, b7

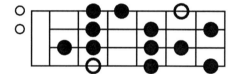

Review your musical goals today.

Note-A-Day
Calendars

Friday
August

3

2007

Choose a song you know how to play well. Play only the left-hand parts (don't worry about whether you can hear the notes or not).

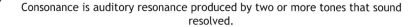

Consonance is auditory resonance produced by two or more tones that sound resolved.

Note-A-Day
Calendars

Saturday
June

2

2007

Improvise, playing the first and fourth strings simultaneously (play the first string with your middle or ring finger and the fourth string with your thumb).

The endpin of the cello is sometimes simply called the pin.

Note-A-Day
Calendars

Thursday
August
2

2007

The V-I chord progression (see the preface) is extremely common in music of all styles. Practice playing and memorizing the sound of a V-I chord progression, e.g., G to C or A to D.

A down-bow is the action of drawing the bow away from the strings.

Sunday
June

3

2007

Improvise using only the index finger on your
left hand (use your right hand as usual).

C minor is considered the key of concentration and solemnity.

Note-A-Day
Calendars

Wednesday
August

1

2007

Choose a song that you can play but have
not yet memorized and memorize it.

Review your musical goals today.

Monday
June
4

2007

Without looking at your cello, name all of the strings and "frets" where the following notes are found (e.g., Db is 4th string-1st "fret", 3rd string-6th "fret", etc.):
G, B, F, Eb

Set your metronome to 60 bpm. Starting from the fourth string and moving one string at a time to the first, say which "fret" the note appears on with each click.

Do this separately with each of the notes above.

Melba toast is named after Australian opera singer Dame Nellie Melba (1861-1931).

Tuesday
July

31

2007

Memorize the following chord qualities and symbols:

suspended second or "sus two" (sus2) (1, 2, 5)
suspended fourth or "sus four" (sus4) (1, 4, 5)

Spell each with A as the root (see the preface).

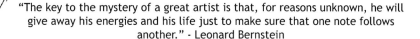

"The key to the mystery of a great artist is that, for reasons unknown, he will
give away his energies and his life just to make sure that one note follows
another." - Leonard Bernstein

Note-A-Day
Calendars

Tuesday
June
5
2007

Play the minor scale below.

Play it again, singing each note as you play it - use the syllables do (1), re (2), mi (3), fa (4), sol (5), la (6), ti (7), do (8), with each syllable corresponding to the note in the scale.

Next, play the root (first) note. Sing the second note (using re), then play the third note. Sing the fourth note (using fa), play the fifth, etc., ascending and descending.

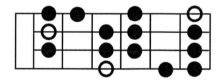

Music was sent down a telephone line for the first time in 1876, the year the phone was invented.

Note-A-Day Calendars

Monday
July
30

2007

Improvise using only the middle finger on your
left hand (use your right hand as usual).

Apocalyptica is a Finnish band consisting of three classically-trained cellists.
Their specialty is heavy metal music on cellos, although they also play classical
music. They started by playing covers of Metallica.

Note-A-Day
Calendars

Wednesday
June

6

2007

Memorize the following chord qualities and symbols:

major seventh (maj7) (1, 3, 5, 7)
minor seventh (m7) (1, b3, 5, b7)

Spell each with A as the root (see the preface).

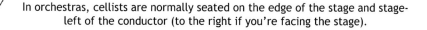

In orchestras, cellists are normally seated on the edge of the stage and stage-left of the conductor (to the right if you're facing the stage).

Sunday
July

29

2007

Some tips for improvising:

- Determine the key and chords you'll be playing over
- Identify where the beat is, and lock into the groove before playing
- Start slowly
- Listen, both to yourself and to the other musicians
- Don't rely too much on theory and technique; relax and trust your intuition
- Be creative
- Take risks; you might discover something new
- Be melodic; if you can sing what you're playing, you're on the right track
- If you make a mistake, play it twice

Heavy metal is a genre of music that emerged in the 1970s. It took a hybrid of blues and rock to create a thick, heavy, guitar-and-drums-centered sound, characterized by the use of highly amplified distortion.

Practice memorizing and playing the following intervals (an interval is the distance between two notes).

minor sixth (m6); 4 steps or 8 "frets"; Example: D to Bb
minor seventh (m7); 5 steps or 10 "frets"; Example: D to C

Play the higher note, then the lower note. Sing both. Play both notes simultaneously. Sing both. Memorize the sound.

m6

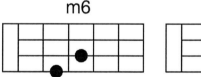

m7

A lute player is called a lutenist.

Saturday
July
28

2007

Memorize the diatonic chords (see the preface) for major keys:

I = Major
ii = minor
iii = minor
IV = Major
V = Major
vi = minor
vii° = diminished

Dissonance is auditory tension produced by two or more tones that sound tense
or unresolved.

Friday
June
8
2007

Put on a recording that you like. Improvise over it
without playing any of the same parts that are on
the recording. Do this for at least one song.

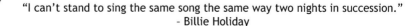

"I can't stand to sing the same song the same way two nights in succession."
- Billie Holiday

Note-A-Day
Calendars

Friday
July
27

2007

Read a current cello magazine from cover to cover. Do not skip anything (including ads, letters, etc.). See what you can learn or discover.

Fresco is a directive to perform a passage in a vigorous, lively, or "fresh" manner.

Note-A-Day
Calendars

Saturday
June
9

2007

Choose a song you can play well. Rearrange the different parts and create a new song out of it (you can switch versus and choruses, move riffs around, repeat some parts more or less times, change the dynamics, etc.).

Bach, Beethoven, and Brahms are known collectively as "The three B's."

Note-A-Day
Calendars

Thursday
July
26

2007

Improvise using only notes on the D string.

The correct position of the bridge is at the center of the f-holes, perpendicular to the body of the cello.

Sunday
June
10

2007

Draw the bow in one direction, starting from the frog and ending at the head. Without pausing, improvise. Once the bow reaches the head, pause, switch strings, then reverse the bowing direction. Again, improvise without pausing.

Continue doing this for at least five minutes.
Vary the speed of bowing.

Stradivari's most famous cello is the "Servais." Made in 1709, it was the last full-scale cello he made.

Wednesday
July
25
2007

Practice the following minor scale in this manner: ascending and descending in half-notes, then quarter-notes, then eighth-notes.

Next, start on the root and skip to the third note in the scale, back to the second note, skip to the fourth, etc., ascending and descending in all of the above rhythms.

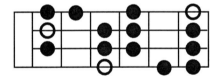

Note-A-Day
Calendars

Monday
June
11

2007

Create various set lists for performing. Create a one-song set list, a 30-minute set list, and a 60-minute set list. Be sure to include time for talking (such as introductions to the songs) and applause.

Experiment with different song sequences, noticing which sequences work the best. Take into account dynamics, speed, style or flavor, popularity, variety, etc. when setting the order. Have an encore song ready as well.

Choose songs that you can play well. If you want to try out newer songs, only choose one or two.

The Baroque period coincided with the birth of opera.

Note-A-Day
Calendars

Tuesday
July
24

2007

Choose three notes. Improvise using only those three notes for five minutes. See how creative and musical you can be.

The lowered 3rd and 7th notes in blues are known as "blue notes."

Tuesday
June

12

2007

Improvise using only your right hand.

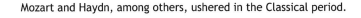

Mozart and Haydn, among others, ushered in the Classical period.

Note-A-Day
Calendars

Monday
July
23
2007

Learn and memorize the names for all the parts
of the cello and bow (see the preface).

"A composer is a guy who goes around forcing his will on unsuspecting air
molecules, often with the assistance of unsuspecting musicians." – Frank Zappa

Play a major scale. While playing the scale, sing the note that is seven notes below the one you are playing (while staying in the scale). Tip: first play the note you'll be singing to learn the pitch, then go back and play the first note while singing the second one.

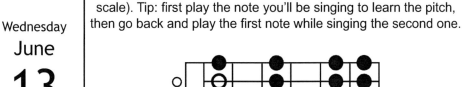

"Syd" Barrett's (Pink Floyd) real name was Roger.

Note-A-Day

Calendars

Sunday
July
22

2007

Play each of the following chords as an arpeggio (one note at a time, in order):

half-diminished or minor seven flat five
(m7b5) (1, b3, b5, b7)

diminished seventh (dim7 or °7)
(1, b3, b5, bb7)

Play each with D as the root (see the preface).
Pay attention to the sound of each arpeggio.

Composer David Popper's etudes are notorious among cellists worldwide. His "High School of Cello Playing" etudes are incredibly difficult, but are used almost universally by advanced cellists to improve their technique.

Memorize how to spell the minor scale (1, 2, b3, 4, 5, b6, b7).

Memorize and play the Eb minor scale on the fourth string only, then play it using the pattern below.

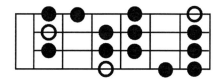

Celli is the correct plural of cello.

Note-A-Day
Calendars

Saturday
July
21

2007

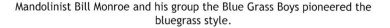

Memorize and learn to play one new chord today.

Use the preface, or visit http://4stringchords.com.

Mandolinist Bill Monroe and his group the Blue Grass Boys pioneered the bluegrass style.

Play the minor pentatonic scale below.

Play it again, singing each note as you play it - use the syllables do (1), mi (3), fa (4), sol (5), ti (7), do (8), with each syllable corresponding to the note in the scale.

Next, play the root (first) note. Sing that note, then sing (without playing) the entire scale, ascending and descending.

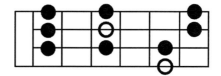

Buffalo Springfield's founders include Stephen Stills and Neil Young.

Practice memorizing and playing the following intervals (an interval is the distance between two notes).

perfect unison (PU); 0 steps or 0 "frets"; Example: G# to G# (same pitch)
perfect octave (PO); 6 steps or 12 "frets"; Example: Eb to Eb

Play the higher note, then the lower note. Sing both. Play both notes simultaneously. Sing both. Memorize the sound.

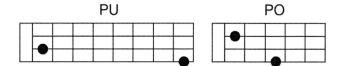

Bitonality refers to a composition where each part (melody and accompaniment, or treble and bass) is in a different key.

Play an "Ab". Improvise using the Ab Aeolian mode for several minutes.

Occasionally play "Ab" or an Abm arpeggio as a reference for your ears.

Saturday
June
16

2007

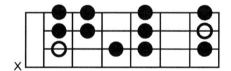

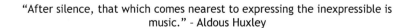

"After silence, that which comes nearest to expressing the inexpressible is music." - Aldous Huxley

Some performance tips:

• Choose music that you like to play.

• Choose a diverse range of songs; vary tempos, keys, moods, etc.

• Play through the whole set beforehand, from start to finish. Include anything you want to say about the pieces, time for applause, etc.

• Set aside plenty of time before performing to set up and relax.

• Create a routine to help you relax immediately before playing, such as breathing, massage, meditation or visualization, etc.

Thursday
July
19
2007

"I've dedicated my life to music so far. And every time I've let it slip and gotten somewhere else, it's showed." - Neil Young

Note-A-Day
Calendars

Sunday
June

17

2007

Choose five notes, and an order in which to play them.

Improvise, keeping the same order. Experiment
with rhythm, volume, and tone.

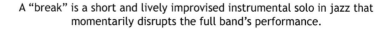

A "break" is a short and lively improvised instrumental solo in jazz that
momentarily disrupts the full band's performance.

Wednesday
July

18

2007

Compile a CD or tape of inspirational cellists and/or cello-oriented songs.

Listen to it regularly for ideas and inspiration.

Actor Alan Rickman took cello lessons for his role in the movie "Truly Madly Deeply." He handled the right (bowing) hand, but the left hand was provided by a real cellist standing behind him, with his arm through Rickman's armpit.

Note-A-Day
Calendars

Monday
June
18

2007

Before practicing, do a relaxation exercise.

Choose one part to begin with. Inhale while squeezing the part tightly, then exhale while relaxing the part.

Do this with your fingers, hands, wrists, forearms, elbows, biceps, shoulders, neck, face, and head. Then move down your body, ending with your feet.

Notice how this affects your playing afterwards.

Domenico Gabrielli of Bologna was the first known composer for the cello.

Note-A-Day

Calendars

Tuesday
July

17

2007

Play a song that you are learning. As you play it, say the name of each note (play it as slowly as you need to).

Scordatura refers to retuning a stringed instrument in order to facilitate playing certain sections of a composition. Often, these sections would be otherwise impossible to play.

Note-A-Day
Calendars

Tuesday
June

19

2007

Improvise using only legato (without breaks between notes; smooth and connected, such as with slurs and slides).

Counterpoint is the term given to two melodies played at once.

Note-A-Day Calendars

Monday
July
16
2007

Practice memorizing and playing the following intervals (an interval is the distance between two notes).

augmented fourth (A4); 3 steps or 6 "frets"; Example: E to A#
diminished fifth (D5-also called tritone); 3 steps or 6 "frets"; Example: E to Bb

Play the higher note, then the lower note. Sing both. Play both notes simultaneously. Sing both. Memorize the sound.

A4/D5

Bb major is the key of fanfares, and of festival and military marches.

Note-A-Day
Calendars

Wednesday
June
20

2007

Memorize and learn to play one new chord today.

Use the preface, or visit http://4stringchords.com.

"I think pure rock and roll, good rock and roll, has the same thing that anything that's pure has—and that's honesty. Unthinking, primal honesty." - Paul Stanley of Kiss

Note-A-Day Calendars

Play an "Eb". Improvise using the Eb Aeolian mode for several minutes.

Occasionally play "Eb" or an Ebm arpeggio as a reference for your ears.

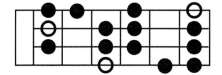

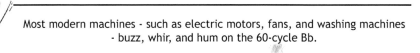

Most modern machines - such as electric motors, fans, and washing machines - buzz, whir, and hum on the 60-cycle Bb.

Figure out (by ear) the melodies of Mary had a Little Lamb, Happy Birthday, and Jingle Bells.

Check out www.AllCoolMusic.com for samples.

The brace is the sign that connects two or more staves, indicating that the parts are to be played simultaneously.

Note-A-Day
Calendars

Saturday
July
14

2007

Practice slides: put your first finger on the fourth string, 3rd "fret" (Eb). Play the note, and slide up to the 4th "fret" (E) while continuing to bow and without lifting your finger. Put your finger back on the previous note (Eb), play, and slide up to the 5th "fret" (F) while bowing.

Continue doing this all the way to the highest note on the string. Practice sliding at different speeds.

Francesco Alborea, known as "Francischello", was the first virtuoso cellist to make an impact on the public. He was also the first to make the cello known in eastern Europe.

Note-A-Day
Calendars

Friday
June

22

2007

What are you sitting on when you practice? Is it comfortable? If not, come up with a solution, such as a pillow, raising or lowering height, using something with a back, etc.

Find something that will keep your thighs parallel to the ground and your back straight. Experiment with different chairs and surfaces, and see what works best.

You may be using a chair or surface out of habit, without having given it much thought. If so, experiment with alternatives.

Benjamin Hallett, a six-year-old English boy, was likely the first child prodigy on the cello. He held his instrument like a double bass.

Note-A-Day
Calendars

Friday
July
13
2007

Make a list of the things you want to practice today. Include how
much time you wish to spend on each area.

Do this each time you practice, and notice
if it helps you stay more focused.

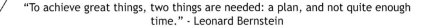

"To achieve great things, two things are needed: a plan, and not quite enough
time." - Leonard Bernstein

Note-A-Day
Calendars

Saturday
June
23

2007

Research a cellist who inspires you. Look in magazines, on the Internet, in books, etc.

Learn how this person became successful. Who did they listen to? What did they practice? What motivated him/her to persist?

Use this information to give you fresh ideas and model their success, while keeping your own originality and style in mind.

Originally, the bows used on stringed instruments were curved like archery bows.

Note-A-Day Calendars

Thursday
July
12
2007

Play the major pentatonic scale below.

Play it again, singing each note as you play it - use the syllables do (1), re (2), mi (3), sol (5), la (6), do (8), with each syllable corresponding to the note in the scale.

Next, play the root (first) note. Sing the second note (using re), then play the third note. Sing the fourth note (using sol), play the fifth, etc., ascending and descending.

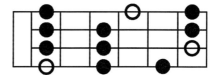

Tom Bethune (1849-1908) was blind and born into slavery, yet he toured the world as a gifted classical pianist.

Sunday
June

24

2007

Play a song you are working on and/or feel challenged by. Do
your best to play it correctly.

Next, try to play it wrong. Notice how this affects your playing - did
you play better or worse than when you tried to get it right?

Now, just play it normally, without trying to get it right
or wrong. Do you notice any differences?

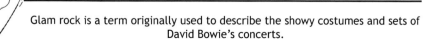

Glam rock is a term originally used to describe the showy costumes and sets of
David Bowie's concerts.

Note-A-Day
Calendars

Wednesday
July
11

2007

Choose three notes, and an order in which to play them.

Improvise, keeping the same order. Experiment
with rhythm, volume, and tone.

Chuck Berry's first hit, "Maybellene," quickly climbed the charts in all three
major categories of that time (R&B, Country, and Popular), an unheard of
achievement.

Note-A-Day
Calendars

Monday
June
25

2007

Practice your air cello!

First, choose a song you are working on and go crazy, jumping around, making faces, etc. Relax and have fun with it.

Play it again, this time playing the parts accurately (move your fingers exactly as you would if you were playing it for real).

Notice how this affects your playing when you actually play the song.

Staccato is Italian for "detached."

Note-A-Day
Calendars

Tuesday
July
10

2007

Improvise using only notes on the G string.

Bernard Heinrich Romberg, regarded as the "father" of the German school of
cello playing, was in a quartet with Beethoven, who admired Romberg's playing.
Romberg, however, found it hard to understand Beethoven's compositions.

Note-A-Day
Calendars

Tuesday
June
26

2007

Play one note for five minutes. Using volume, timbre (tone), rhythm, vibrato, bowing techniques, etc., experiment with how much expression you can get out of it.

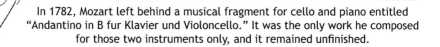

In 1782, Mozart left behind a musical fragment for cello and piano entitled "Andantino in B fur Klavier und Violoncello." It was the only work he composed for those two instruments only, and it remained unfinished.

Note-A-Day
Calendars

Monday
July
9

2007

Create a special practice space. If you already have one, see how you can improve it. Make it organized, easy to access, private, clean, inspirational (using posters or inspiring objects), and comfortable.

"Music is religion for me. There'll be music in the hereafter, too." – Jimi Hendrix

Note-A-Day
Calendars

Wednesday
June
27

2007

Recall your past performances, or, if you've never performed, what you imagine performing would be like.

Think back to (or imagine) the best performance. How did you feel? What did you play? What were the circumstances and conditions, such as location, audience size and demographics, temperature, atmosphere, etc.?

Take a minute and picture it in as much detail as possible, and notice how your body feels.

Now think back to the worst performance, again considering the previous questions.

What can you learn from comparing the two to make future experiences more enjoyable and successful?

"Count" Basie's real name was William.

Note-A-Day
Calendars

Sunday
July
8

2007

Put your first finger on the 3rd string-4th "fret". Touch the string, but do not press down. When you play the string, it shouldn't ring (it should sound "dead" or muted).

Continue playing the string while SLOWLY pressing your finger down, until the note clearly rings.

STOP PRESSING! Notice how little pressure it takes to make the note ring clearly; any more pressure is a waste of energy.

Practice this using different fingers on different "frets" and strings.

Irving Berlin never learned to formally read or write music.

Note-A-Day
Calendars

Thursday
June
28

2007

Create a daily practice log. Keep track of what you practice, how long you practice each thing, and areas to develop, along with any other useful information to help you track your progress.

Check back periodically to see how you've progressed.

Beams are the horizontal lines connecting adjacent notes.

Note-A-Day
Calendars

Saturday
July
7

2007

Find sheet music for another instrument and play it on the cello, or find recorded music for another instrument and learn it on the cello.

Beethoven tried to find a remedy for his deafness by using "scientific" medications of that era, including experimenting with treatments of "sulfur vapor," mercury, and a vibration machine.

Note-A-Day
Calendars

Friday
June
29

2007

Memorize the following chord qualities:

major ninth (maj9) (1, 3, 5, 7, 9)
minor ninth (m9) (1, b3, 5, b7, 9)

Spell each with A as the root (see the preface).

"Do it again on the next verse, and people will think you meant it." – Chet Atkins

Regardless of how technically advanced you are, playing with conviction is one of the most important skills that a musician can learn. You can make "wrong" notes sound good if you play them with conviction.

Choose a simple riff or phrase, and practice playing it over and over again. Play it like you really mean it, without worrying how it sounds or trying to get it right. Relax and have fun with it - make faces, move around as you play it, and act like you are the master of this particular riff.

Add some "wrong" notes, and see if you can still sound convincing. It matters more how you play than what you play.

Friday

July

6

2007

Melora Creager, of the cello-band Rasputina, was a touring cellist with Nirvana, and played with many other popular artists, including Belle and Sebastian and the Pixies.

Note-A-Day
Calendars

Saturday
June

30

2007

Watch a movie or show and play along with it,
creating your own soundtrack to what's happening
on the screen. If it helps, turn off the volume.

An extension means to widen the hand from its normal position in order to reach
higher or lower notes.

Note-A-Day
Calendars

Thursday
July
5

2007

Memorize the relative minor keys for each of the major keys below. Both keys share the same notes, but different ones are emphasized in each (such as the root).

C major - A minor

G major - E minor

D major - B minor

A major - F# minor

E major - C# minor

B major - G# minor

Beethoven was guardian to his two younger brothers.

Sunday
July

1

2007

As a warm-up exercise, practice the following finger patterns on one string on adjacent notes.

Choose one pattern at a time and play it at least four times in a row. Use a metronome, and play as sixteenth-notes (four notes per click of the metronome). Start slowly!

1-2-3-4
1-3-2-4
1-4-2-3
1-2-4-3

Review your musical goals today.

Wednesday
July
4

2007

Improvise, playing the third and fourth strings simultaneously
(play the third string with your index or middle finger and
the fourth string with your thumb, or both using the bow).

The invention of the term and technique of bebop is generally attributed to
Dizzie Gillespie.

Monday
July
2

2007

Play a major scale. While playing the scale, sing the note that is two notes below the one you are playing (while staying in the scale). Tip: first play the note you'll be singing to learn the pitch, then go back and play the first note while singing the second one.

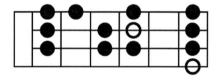

Lightly touching the string with a fingertip at a harmonic node (for example, halfway or one-third along the length of a string) while bowing close to the bridge will produce harmonics.

Tuesday
July
3
2007

Practice the following Ionian mode (major scale) pattern in this manner: ascending and descending in half-notes, then quarter-notes, then eighth-notes.

Next, start on the root and skip to the third note in the scale, back to the second note, skip to the fourth, etc., ascending and descending in all of the above rhythms.

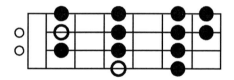

The Beach Boys' "Good Vibrations" took months to record and was said to cost $1,000,000 in studio time to create.